LE CORBUSIER

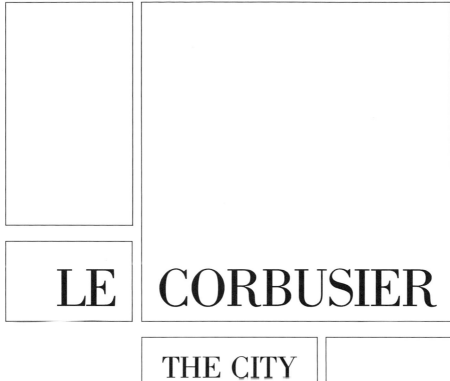

LE CORBUSIER

THE CITY OF REFUGE PARIS 1929/33

by BRIAN BRACE TAYLOR

with an Introduction by Kenneth Frampton

The University of Chicago Press ■ *Chicago and London*

BRIAN BRACE TAYLOR is professor of history and theory at the Ecole
d'Architecture Paris-Belleville and executive editor of *Mimar* magazine.

The University of Chicago Press, Chicago 60637
The University of Chicago Press, Ltd., London
© 1987 by The University of Chicago
All rights reserved. Published 1987
Printed in the United States of America
96 95 94 93 92 91 90 89 88 87   54321

Library of Congress Cataloging-in-Publication Data

Taylor, Brian Brace.
    Le Corbusier, the City of Refuge, Paris 1929–33.

    1. Le Corbusier, 1887–1965—Criticism and interpreta-
tion.   2. Cité de refuge (Paris, France)   3. Asylums—
France—Paris.   4. Salvation Army—France—Paris—
Buildings.   5. Paris (France)—Buildings, structures,
etc.   I. Title.
NA1053.J4T39   1987   725′.55′0924   87-10946
ISBN 0-226-79134-3

Previously published as *La Cité de Refuge di Le Corbusier 1929/33* (Rome: Officina
Edizioni, 1978) and *Le Corbusier: La Cité de Refuge, Paris 1929/33* (Paris:
Equerre, 1980).

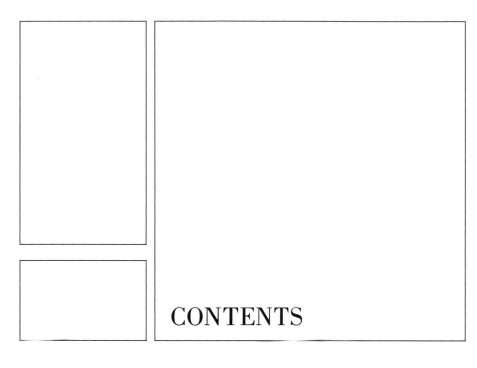

CONTENTS

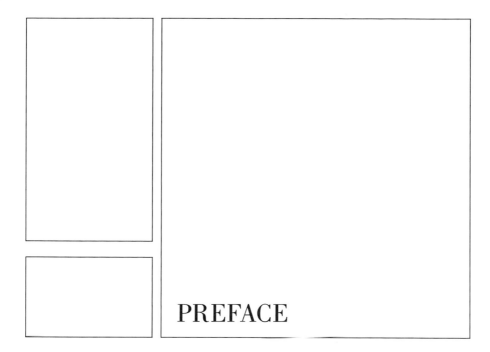

PREFACE

■ This detailed study of a single building, one of the lesser known monuments of modern architecture, first came about as a specific request from an Italian colleague and friend, Professor Giorgo Ciucci, of the Institute of History, Faculty of Architecture, in Venice. It was conceived in 1975 as one of a series of books directed by Professor Ciucci, with the intention of bringing into focus the lives of such buildings from conception through construction to actual utilization. Although originally published in Italian (1978) and subsequently in French (1980), the contents have served a few specialists of le Corbusier (not always with proper acknowledgement) as well as students of architecture who sought thorough documentation—sketches, scale drawings, photographs—of one history-making edifice. For indeed, from the outset a primary goal was to provide a pedagogical tool that would illuminate the various factors influencing a building's design, especially the workings of a great creative mind.

In the last fifteen years a new type of historical scholarship has emerged, one that attempts to go into greater depth of analysis, particularly with regard to the socioeconomic and political context of individual works, than the more general, comprehensive histories. This movement of historians has, for instance, taken up the tools of structuralist analysis, or investigated the intricate relationship between building typologies and the morphology of specific urban fabrics. The author wishes to acknoweldge the strong influence upon this book of architect-historians Bernard Huet, Manfredo Tafuri, and Kenneth Frampton. When more of these monographic studies have been produced, placing emphasis not so much upon the finished product as upon the processes by which such complex works came into existence, there will be better opportunities for reevaluating the larger significance of these monuments within an overall history of modern architecture.

BRIAN BRACE TAYLOR

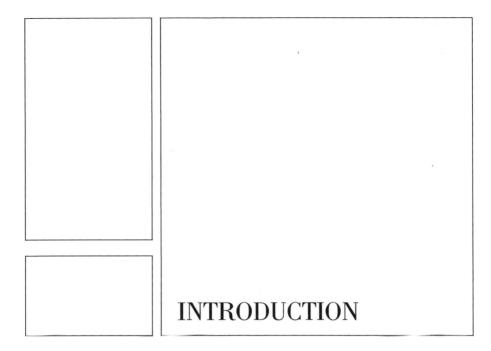

INTRODUCTION

■ There is surely no building in Le Corbusier's renowned and, by now, well-documented life that caused so much controversy and sensation as the Salvation Army's Cité de Refuge that he designed and realized in Paris between June 1929 and December 1933. And while there were at least three other equally ambitious buildings realized by Le Corbusier and Pierre Jeanneret over the same period, only this work came into being as a *cause célèbre*, and it has, in many respects, remained a controversial building ever since. This stormy, almost scandalous reputation seems to derive from two main causes: first, the idiosyncratic, social-reformist client for whom the building was built (a client who proffered a brief that resembled in many respects both the Fourierist phalanstery and the "social condensers" of the young Soviet Union), and second, the generally underdeveloped state of the French building industry in the early thirties. One has to add to this, of course, Le Corbusier's own avant gardist predisposition to interpret every brief as an occasion on which to demonstrate the coming into being of the "new society" and the "new man"; his desire, that is, not only to project an entirely unprecedented socio-spatial organization but also to express its form in the most advanced technologies available. In the last analysis, perhaps, the scandal, such as it is, stems from here.

This study is, in many ways, a conscious act of demystification, and it is to be valued in that regard in its own right, since it is, in this single respect, virtually unique. As far as I know, there have been no other studies to date, in which an acclaimed work of architecture has been analyzed in all its social and productive aspects down, as it were, to the last nail and the penultimate architect's change order. Moreover, Taylor's Marxist-influenced, demystifying analysis (he has been strongly affected in this regard by the work of Michel Foucault) operates on two levels simultaneously. The first of these could be classed as a Neo-Structuralist critique of the Salvation Army as a reformist institution, particularly in the light of Foucault's revelatory work on hospitals and penal institutions—his studies entitled *Discipline and Punishment* and *Madness and Civilization*. Indeed, the term *heterotopia* owes its modern critical coinage to these works, and it is no accident that this essay, researched and written in Paris in the late sixties and early seventies, should have been strongly affected by Foucault's insights into the role and nature of particular sociocultural institutions, isolated from the rest of society.

It is significant that Le Corbusier was influenced (not to say haunted) by the image of just such a heterotopia from the very beginning of his career; not only by the model of the monastery and the monastic way of life, but also by Charles Fourier's utopian socialist vision of a people's palace cum collective dwelling that Le Corbusier saw as the ideal heterotopic community. Owing to the longevity of this concept, we must recognize that the realization of Unite d'Habitation at Marseille in 1952 was a building-out, in the fact, of a Fourierist paradigm in modern terms. Le Corbusier's intentions are hardly altered by the fact that this utopian community remained a myth and that in most respects, it failed to come into being. What is important for us here, is that he approached the commission for the Cité de Refuge in very similar terms. Although Taylor remarks on the coincidence between the heterotopic brief of the Salvation Army and Le Corbusier's preoccupation with the collective dwelling, he fails to acknowledge sufficiently the Fourierist ideology that wears an integral part of Le Corbusier's own reformist repertoire, dating back to his very early years as a teaching assistant in the school of La Chaux-de-Fonds. Taylor does indicate, however, the general influence of the Soviet constructivists and, above all, the direct influence of Moses Ginsburg's Narkomfin block erected in Moscow between 1928 and 1930, a "social condenser" that was completed just at the time when Le Corbusier was designing the Cité de Refuge.

Taylor's attitude to Le Corbusier is critical to say the least, and, far from indulging in the hero-worship that has characterized, in some way or another, most of the studies of this, his centennial year, Taylor takes the grand master of the heroic period apart on almost every count, ranging from his naive attitude toward technology to his incapacity to provide adequate site supervision; from his continual belatedness in keeping up with the production schedule, to his stubborn refusal to comply with building regulations of the city. He is particularly harsh on him for his refusal to recognize the intolerable "greenhouse effect" brought about by his installation of an unshielded curtain-wall, facing due south; a recalcitrant attitude that he was finally to modify once ideology changed after the Second World War. Finally, Taylor takes Le Corbusier to task for his politics, for his political opportunism, veering towards fascism, as he became increasingly disillusioned with the left and fell under the influence of the syndicalist editors of *Plans* and *Preludes*, Herbert Langadelle and Phillipe Lamour. One can hardly fault Taylor about any of this, although one may, at times, feel that his tone is somewhat censorious, to the point of being biased, particularly from the point of view of making a balanced cultural and political judgment of the period as a whole.

Be this as it may, the Cité de Refuge is a seminal work from many points of view, above all, perhaps, because it is one of the most "machinist" works of Le Corbusier's career. This is the house as a "machine for living" taken to its theoretical extreme. And yet there is evidence to suggest that 1933, the year that the Cité de Refuge was finally completed, is the last year that Le Corbusier maintained his faith in the progressive destiny of the machine-age civilization. It is apt and ironic that this flawed "building-machine" should come to be the last machinist work of his life, although this abandonment of the "machine" as an ideal and as an icon was not a direct outcome of the failure of the work. Indeed, on the face of it, at its unveiling the work was a brilliant tectonic and artistic success. In fact, the main technical "flaw"—namely, the air-conditioning—was not entirely Le Corbusier's fault. It stemmed as much from injudicious cuts in the budget (the clients refused to install a double-layered curtain wall with a "plenium" void between) and the relatively undeveloped state of air-conditioning as an art, as it did from Le Corbusier's stubborn "ideological" approach to technology and sun control. It is interesting to note, in passing, that the curtain-wall of his Maison Clarté, Geneva, built at approximately the same time, was equipped with external roller shutters and blinds as opposed to the drapes installed just inside the curtain-wall of the Cité de Refuge. As Taylor observes, Le Corbusier was intent on proving a general paradigm with this work, and this compulsion to reveal, as it were, the glistening shape of the brave new world, took priority over other considerations. Like other pioneers, he was convinced that he was prophetic, and we have to admit that, in the last analysis, he was, in that hermetic, air-conditioned, high-rise structures, faced entirely in heat-resistant glass, became elements of normative practice twenty years later.

Taylor shows us how this was a work carried out against considerable odds, on an extremely difficult site and in total opposition to (where not in contravention of) the laws governing standard Parisian building practice, dating from the high Haussmannian period. It says everything, in this regard, that the architects inclined the principal south facade by forty centimeters in five floors, in order to meet the cornice, set-back, datum for the *garabit* required by the regulations!

Aside from all this, one has to concede the formal brilliance of the *parti*, that is to say, the fact that the awkwardness of the entry, given the necessity of entering from a narrow frontage to one end of a transverse site, has been solved by a series of quite remarkable transitions, between the somewhat attenuated approach and the principal vertical access of the building which, to all intents and purposes, is displaced toward the other end of the site. This "still life" assembly of Platonic forms affords the possibility of a rite of passage between the initial threshold and the actual reception of inmates into the building. There is a very subtle, hierarchic shift in the representational modes here in which, while the *porte cochere* serves as the emblematic monument of the institution (a cube plus a golden rectangular prism), the cylindrical form represents and accommodates the primary foyer of the refuge as a whole. It is surely a gesture of great plastic facility and daring that those two elements are separated by a "flying" bridge and free-standing portico plane, made out of welded metal.

There are many metaphors and paradigmatic themes that are not immediately apparent in this work, above all, perhaps, the fact that Le Corbusier insisted on calling the work a Cité de Refuge, as though, like the Carthusian monastic type by which he was obsessed, it was to be seen as an urban microcosm in itself (heterotopia). It was, in any event, like his contemporaneous Pavillon Suisse built in the Cité Universitaire, Paris, a realization of a fragment of his standard "*bloc à redent*" (complete with the continuous curtain-wall or *pan verre*) that he was to project between 1930 and 1934, as the normative residential building type of his new radiant city—see his book, *La Ville Radieuse*, published in 1934. Indeed, as Taylor remarks, in 1932 he projected a *redent*-like extension of the Cité de Refuge, in which its slab form was to be linked to a whole campus of facilities that he referred to as a Cité d'Hébergement. (In other publications Le Corbusier refers to this complex as a Cité d'Hospitalière, implying that it might also have been developed as a health facility.)

This was, in many respects, the ultimate work of an era, for, henceforth, his ideological/architectonic position dramatically shifts. The invention of the *brise soleil* (sun breaker) in his Durand project for Algiers, in the very year that the Cité de Refuge is completed, amounts to a watershed in his career, for, from now on, he is to be preoccupied with achieving a more organic and realistic balance between archaic form and modern technology; between, as it were, the shielding depth of the traditional wall and the transparent lightness of the skeleton frame. The bitter lesson, so to speak, of the Cité de Refuge was to be immediately assimilated.

KENNETH FRAMPTON

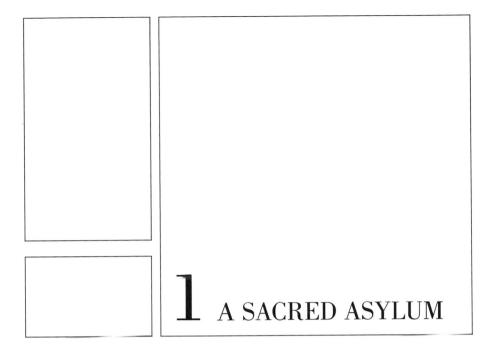

1 A SACRED ASYLUM

> ■ We proclaim integration; and we maintain that the ideal of society—that is, the state towards which society is already marching—is a society of integrated, combined labor. A society where each individual is a producer of both manual and intellectual work; where each able-bodied human being is a worker, and where each worker works both in the field and the industrial workshop; where every aggregation of resources—it may be a nation, or rather a region—produces and itself consumes most of its own agricultural and manufactured produce.[1]

These lines, first written in the late 1880s in a series of articles published in England by the renowned political economist and anarchist Peter Kropotkin, summarize the essential points of numerous subsequent schemes proposed by other would-be reformers of contemporary industrialized society. While echoes of Kropotkin's theses concerning decentralization of industries and the creation of industrial villages are better known to students of urban history through the works of Ebenezer Howard,[2] there was yet another, prior scheme for social reform based upon principles similar to Kropotkin's; it was set forth in a book (published in 1890) entitled *In Darkest England, and the Way Out* by General William Booth (1829–1912), founder of the Salvation Army.[3] In contrast to Howard's proposals, and even to many utopian socialist schemes earlier in the century, William Booth's program had the significant advantage that a number of the practical measures which he advocated had already been initiated at the time he published his "Grand Scheme."

1

The "Grand Scheme" of General Booth

One should mention at the very outset, before entering into the details, the class of persons for whom this program was intended as a means for achieving well-being. The organization which he founded in Great Britain in 1865 and of which he was the supreme commander was an evangelical protestant religious sect, which sought to alleviate the physical misery and suffering of the most disinherited, degraded, and outcast members of society, aiming at the same time to work a religious conversion upon those who accepted their aid. It is necessary to keep this restricted scope of the Salvation Army's efforts in mind, since the economic and social reforms proposed, in many ways very novel and even progressive for their time, were directed towards a category of persons who were essentially without property, without money or privilege, and were hence the most vulnerable victims of capitalist industrial societies. This mechanism for reform, while also serving as a model of an ideal organization of society for its more privileged members, was nevertheless aimed at the reintegration of the lowest classes of the population into the existing economic framework.

Seventy years ago George Bernard Shaw, the Irish playwright and Fabian Socialist, wrote his celebrated play about the Salvation Army entitled *Major Barbara*, manifesting what he believed to be the Army's essentially partisan political role, wishing to mediate between the poor and the rest of society.

Walk through the poorer quarters of our cities on a Sunday when the men are not working, but resting and chewing the cud of their reflections. You will find one expression common to every mature face: the expression of cynicism. They have found that every man has his price; and they have been foolishly or corruptly taught to mistrust and despise him for the necessary and salutary condition of existence. When they learn that General Booth, too, has his price, they do not admire him because it is a high one, and admit the need of organizing society so that he shall get it in an honorable way: they conclude that his character is unsound and that all religious men are hypocrites and allies of their sweaters and oppressors. They know that the large subscriptions which help to support the Army are endowments, not of religion but of the wicked doctrine of docility in poverty and humility under oppression. . . .

. . . Churches are suffered to exist only on the condition that they preach submission to the State as at present capitalistically organised. . . . And this is why no tolerated Church or Salvation Army can ever win the entire confidence of the poor. It must be on the side of the police and the military, no matter what it believes or disbelieves. . . . Indeed the religious bodies, as the almoners of the rich, become a sort of auxiliary police, taking off the insurrectionary edge of poverty with coals and blankets, bread and treacle, and soothing and cheering the victims with hopes of immense and inexpensive happiness in another world when the process of working them to a premature death in the service of the rich is complete in this.[4]

Whether one accepts Shaw's scathing condemnation of the Salvation Army as just or not, we must nevertheless keep in mind Booth's own candid assertion that his was *not* a revolutionary enterprise; and that while he had learned a great deal from the programs and experiences of other nineteenth-century reform movements, his Scheme did not aim at a radical or violent restructuring of existing socioeconomic relationships.[5]

The principal thrust of his plan aimed at a spiritual transformation in the individual, and, by the same token, at improving his social worth through adherence to a concrete program. This approach was essentially that echoed in Le Corbusier's discourse of the 1930s, in his *Response to Moscow*,[6] articles in the periodical *Plans*, or in *The Radiant City* (1935).[7] Redemption of the individual for Christianity, and for society in general, was called for because economic conditions and unemployment in the modern industrialized world had victimized and brutalized men. What makes Booth's Scheme interesting is that he advocated a comprehensive and permanent solution to the evil of unemployment, which was the cause of misery among the urban proletariat. But as he explicitly made clear, his program for aiding the "prisoners of society, who are the sick and wounded in our hospitals" must be operative within the existing system: "While assisting one class of the community it must not seriously interfere with the interest of another."[8]

Curing the misery perpetrated by unemployment involved quite simply putting the individual back to work, of giving him a "calling," which had been a major ethical tenet of Protestantism since the time of Calvin.[9] Starting from the basic premise of assistance through work as the means for achieving personal salvation and attenuating family and class conflicts, William Booth elaborated a vast economic mechanism (which he himself likened to the functioning of a machine) that would take persons off the streets, reform them, and (in the final stage) send them back into the world as enthusiastic converts and "colony builders." When we read the details of the Scheme, success of which had been in large measure postulated upon an authoritarian form of organization and industrial and commercial free enterprise, we perceive quite clearly the essentially similar aims of the Salvation Army and contemporary British imperialism: the one, exploiting the "raw materials" at home, prepared future productive agents for the large-scale capitalist markets of the other.

William Booth published his Scheme in 1890, some twenty-five years after his founding of the Salvation Army. Thus, his proposal had the merit of being, in part, the result of practical experiences over time. He insisted frequently in his writings on the necessity for finding immediate practical solutions to the woes induced by unemployment, and he set forth three fundamental needs: food, shelter, and employment. William Booth began by setting up Cheap Food Depots in the slums of London, three of which were in operation by 1888, and five overnight hostels (Shelters). However, he believed that the *free* distribution of these goods or services, as pursued by most existing philanthropic institutions, required no effort, no commitment from the recipient, thereby precluding any reform of his socioeconomic status. Therefore Booth included workshops as a third key facility in his Scheme, where men and women could earn enough money to pay for meals and lodging in a Salvation Army Restaurant and Shelter. These three organisms constituted what he called his City Colonies in urban areas.

With "Work for All" his slogan and keystone in the arch representing the Salvation Army's social campaign, Booth proposed a variety of ways for putting the unemployed to work. Much of it was based upon what it is fashionable today to call the *recycling* of waste materials. The most famous of his programs was the Household Salvage Brigade, concerned with restoring or reutilizing in a different form the rubbish thrown away by city dwellers: food, clothing, paper, furniture, utensils, and so on. Then there were to be workshops for transforming old sardine tins into toys, for repairing shoes and umbrellas, for washing and recycling bottles. In sum, the system was intended to employ the human "debris" (if we may use the term) of the capitalist wage-system, as Booth called it, to transform the debris collected from those who were better off.

A Farm Colony constituted a second unit in General Booth's vast reform program. Surplus labor accumulating in the City Colony was to be returned to cultivate the land, "the source of all food." The significant feature of this second community is that, as a concept, it echoes the prevalent nineteenth-century theme of a return to nature (paradise) as the means to alleviate the misery and suffering of urban existence. Workers who had demonstrated spiritual and moral progress, and whose talents were needed in the agricultural community, were sent out of the city. While Booth recommended the establishment of an experimental cooperative farm and of industrial villages (à la Kro-

1. Pictorial diagram of the Salvation Army's social works program. (From *In Darkest England* by William Booth, London, 1890)

potkin), it is important to remember that it remained linked to the City Colony in a relationship of interdependence: the city collected food for nourishing pigs, collected bones to be ground into fertilizer, and so forth, while the farms sent food grown on Salvation Army estates into the city for the soup kitchens. Simply as an indication of the emphasis placed upon individual self-reliance and mutual aid within the organization, Booth insisted that the future settlers would have at their disposal all the talent necessary for brick-making and the construction and furnishing of the future farmhouses.[10]

Finally, the Farm Colony was to serve as a training school and testing ground for emigrants who would be sent abroad in order to create Overseas Colonies. The religious missionary role of the Salvation Army was, of course, a factor in the desire to undertake a civilizing activity in foreign lands; however, it should be kept in mind that Booth was living in an age of imperialist expansion, when Great Britain was conquering new sources of materials and new market outlets. This explains how Booth could say:

> The constant travelling of the Colonists backwards and forwards to England makes it absurd to speak of the Colonies as if they were a foreign land. They are simply pieces of Britain distributed about the world, enabling the Britisher to have access to the richest parts of the earth.[11]

He was in favor of the voluntary transfer of the surplus population of England to countries such as Australia, South Africa, and the United States in order that they should be able to have greater possibilities for making a living than in their own industrialized, overcrowded country.

The Salvation Army in France

The Salvation Army arrived in Catholic France in the year 1881 with Miss Catherine Booth, one of William Booth's daughters, at the head of a mission. As in other countries (Catholic or otherwise) where the Army descended for the first time, their initial reception was frequently hostile and even physically threatening—to the point of being thrown in jail, as happened in Boston. Nonetheless, the mission to set up an outpost in France was already sufficiently successful by 1885 to permit General Booth himself to travel to this country.[12] In that year he was invited into the home of fifteen-year-old Albin Peyron (1870–1944) in Nimes, whose father had himself given up a successful business career to devote himself and his fortune to the Salvation Army. Albin Peyron, subsequently to become the Commissioner for all of France and Belgium, was perhaps the most important figure in the history of the Salvation Army in France because of the tremendous social welfare and building campaigns he initiated between 1920 and 1934.[13]

Two noteworthy characteristics of the Salvation Army's history in general are reflected in what occurred in France. First, the fact that Protestantism was a minority religious group did not automatically exclude believers from positions of public power and authority; on the contrary, even today in France, certain branches of the administration are predominantly Protestant fiefs. Naturally, this clannishness on the part of religious minorities in a given locale, stemming from an instinct of self-preservation, has resulted in frequent intermarriage among families of co-believers. A second distinct characteristic of the Salvation Army is the degree of intermarriage among co-Salvationists. The daughter of Albin Peyron married Wycliffe Booth, the grandson of General Booth, for example. Moreover, successive generations of the same family following the Salvationist calling is quite widespread; the present director of the Cité de Refuge in Paris is the son of the Commissioner's chief bookkeeper at the time the building was constructed. This phenomenon is undoubtedly due to the strict confessional beliefs, the evangelical dimension of Salvationist's work, and the military-like discipline imposed from the beginning by patriarch-founder William Booth.

In the period immediately following World War I, the Salvation Army pursued a vigorous and diversified program of social work on a national scale in France, with an efficiency and persistence that put to shame many public administrations. With extremely limited financial means, personnel (149 officers in 70 posts or outposts), and building stock—but benefiting from Peyron's creative leadership—the Salvation Army focused its aid upon the proletariat of the major industrial areas of France, in Lille, Valenciennes, Saint-Étienne, Mulhouse, Paris, Lyon, and Marseille. Hostels for men and women were created; reception centers for soldiers, workers' foyers, workers' restaurants, clothing centers, and orphanages were among their many activities; a "caravan of Salvation" was even organized which visited war-devastated areas of the countryside with needed supplies.

The Salvation Army's bimonthly newspaper En Avant (Forward), which began in 1882, provides the best insights into the dynamic achievements of this period. First of all, the Salvation Army was particularly concerned by the situation of women, abandoned by their husbands or family, who came to them for aid; already in 1920 a foyer (hostel) for young girls had been founded in the Paris suburb of Asnières, and a second one in the fourteenth arrondissement of the capital a year later. The Palais du Peuple, endowed subsequently by the Princess de Polignac, benefactor of the Cité de Refuge, with an annex designed by Le Corbusier, was inaugurated in 1925. An immense fund-raising campaign during 1926 terminated in the acquisition and renovation of an edifice in Paris renamed the Palais de la Femme, which could accommodate eight hundred women. And in succeeding years, other Army-run establishments opened their doors in Paris and in the provinces: an asylum for the aged, the barge-asylum on the Seine (Paris, 1930) transformed by Le Corbusier, a home for delinquent women in 1932 in Peyron's hometown of Nîmes, and of course, the Cité de Refuge in Paris in 1933.

These different social enterprises, founded upon the double premise of "salvation of men by the power of the Holy Spirit" and their readaptation to (or reintegration into) the social system through work, gained much publicity and support within the French Establishment, in large part due to the personality of Albin Peyron. While to manifest a good conscience by the encouragement of *private* financing of social works was altogether in the French tradition (one need only recall, for example, the history of subsidized mass housing[14]) it is nonetheless remarkable that a private organization of this sort, with so few means and so few inherited social advantages, should have several successive ministers as members of the committees of patronage (e.g., Henri Poincaré, Justin Godart), and could invite the President of the Republic to inaugurate a new building. This can be explained—and illustrated in more concrete terms—by the degree to which the public authorities relied upon the Salvation Army for services that they could not provide themselves in 1925: the director of the Petite Roquette prison proposed that the Palais du Peuple temporarily lodge newly released prisoners; the Préfet of Police also asked them to house minors aged thirteen to eighteen years who were picked up on the streets.[15] In one sense, Le Corbusier was ultimately given the opportunity to cope with the brief for a Cité de Refuge precisely because it was a private organization, and not a public one, that was providing many of the services at the time. The Salvation Army and the Cité de Refuge continue to this day to respond to requests for social services from the community.[16]

Ideological Sympathies between Le Corbusier and the Salvation Army

It would perhaps be opportune to ask what precisely was the conception of social community shared by Le Corbusier, the architect, and his client the Salvation Army. It is perfectly conceivable that there was no common ground whatsoever ideologically. Le Corbusier became distinctly more sensitive to the social and political dimensions of architecture and urban planning at the end of the 1920s and in the early 1930s. His writings are one indication of this. When we look to see where he was traveling at the end of the 1920s and with which political authorities he had the greatest contact (aside from South America), we find that it was with the Soviet Union, as client for the largest of his commissions to date, the Centrosoyus, that Le Corbusier was most regularly in touch on a firsthand basis. While his ideas on architecture and urban planning had recieved a favorable hearing among such avant-garde Soviet professionals as the Vesnin brothers, Moses Ginsburg, and Miliutin during his visits to Moscow, the flirtation between Le Corbusier and his Russian colleagues was abruptly ended by, of all things, the "authority" of Stalinist policies after 1932. It was also the era when the Nazis were coming to power in Germany, and when other Western European governments were having to face the social and political consequences of the worldwide economic crisis. Le Corbusier through his personal as well as professional activities was directly in touch with both fascist and syndicalist circles in France, and it is not unusual that his thinking in turn reflected these crises.

With regard to the transformation of society, Le Corbusier's position evolved significantly in the course of the late 1920s and early 1930s, being very much a reflection of certain liberal and radical philosophies prevalent at the time. Insight into these and the architect's espousal of them in one way or another is provided by recent research into that period of French history.[17] The language, concepts, and slogans of leading members of such politico-economic movements as the neosyndicalists, advocating technology and speculating on a republic of producers, permeate much of Le Corbusier's own theories. Rationalization was a central theme "in the air" at the time, and the architect-builder courted industrialists, businessmen-managers, and politicians alike who shared his reformist attitudes toward a capitalist economy and society.

How could he then associate both with a Soviet intellectual avant-garde and with such right-wing neosyndicalists as Georges Valois or capitalist reformers as Ernest Mercier and the Redressement Français? Not to mention the Salvation Army? The answer, it would seem, lies in shared beliefs in such ideas as rationalization, hierarchical organization of decision-making, orderly planned production—in short, technocracy as a means to social progress. Le Corbusier did *not* believe—as did the Soviets—that a *revolutionary* transformation of social relationships must necessrily precede material progress.

Nevertheless, in the period which covers the actual construction of the Cité de Refuge from 1929 to late 1933, a perceptible shift in his

2. The Salvation Army's Palais de la Femme, located at the corner of rue de Charonne and rue Faidherbe in Paris.

3. Le Corbusier, Palais du Peuple, rue des Cordeliers, Paris, 1926. View from the court.

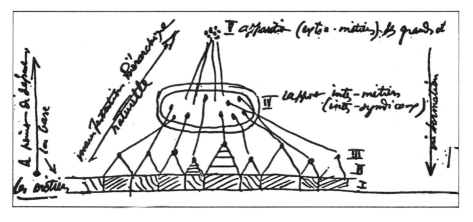

4. Diagram of the regionalist-syndicalist system of government based on "*metier*" unions. (From *La Villa Radieuse*, Le Corbusier, 1935)

5. Le Corbusier with Soviet architects, circa 1930. Kolli in right foreground, Vesnin brothers at left. Archives FLC.

thinking and writing did occur and became more pronounced as time went on. Although he acted as an editor for the periodicals *Plans* (1931–32) and *Preludes* (1933–39), which were monthly publications of the central committee for regional syndicalist activity, Le Corbusier aligned himself with what has been termed *planisme*[18] in economic and social development. This trend was, like the previous ones, often animated by managers and engineers, but also "nonconformist intellectuals" such as himself, who cultivated a highly spiritual and moralistic approach.[19] What is interesting is the way in which this so-called neoliberal planning tendency shaded off into *corporatism* as well. Too adept to allow himself to be labeled politically, the architect nonetheless must be seen as becoming more socially conservative in the 1930s, sympathizing as he had previously with syndicalist values, including organization by producers' competence and training (*metier*). It is probably coincidental but altogether apt that in the course of fund-raising for the Cité de Refuge in 1932 the Salvation Army created an association of donors called "La Corporation des Maçons de la *Cité*" and published a woodcut engraving (by an artist named Wilbo) of a mason in their magazine *En Avant* (13 February 1932); the contribution of money for the Cité's completion allowed you membership in this medieval-like guild, your rank depending upon how much you contributed. Albeit a ploy by the client, it nevertheless symbolizes to a certain degree Le Corbusier's conservatism.

The architect's political thinking was based upon the idea of a supreme authority who, by his ascendance through a hierarchical structure, had been selected as the most competent, natural policymaker for society and would therefore be able to put into effect the plans evolved by specialists (illus. 4). He wrote in 1931 to Edouard Herriot, a prominent radical in French politics, along these same lines, and several months later published an article himself in *Plans* in which he defined his ideology of progress.

Classify and establish a program. Analyze the situation. Make productive decisions. Create order, maintain order by constant vigilance, by constant action, by humanitarian concern and the firmness of a father, and administer, that is to say, know how to take responsibility, to take action instead of sitting back, to be interested in life instead of money, to improve the situation and explain things clearly to people, to erect a balanced program. . . . Authority! Create a program, work on a program, and then achieve it. Spread the benefits of order.[20]

What kind of order, what kind of program? The polemical style and ideological vagaries of Le Corbusier's discourse amount to a kind of smokescreen that makes it impossible to discern where his political

allegiance might lie—although it does not conceal his strongly moralistic strain nor his sympathy for the Vichy government.

It would seem safe to conclude that it was precisely this aspect,
rather than the religious one, that made Le Corbusier sympathetic to
the ideals of the Salvationist movement, which had a program and a
strongly hierarchical basis of authority.

6. From a fund-raising advertisement published in the Salvation Army's newspaper *En Avant*, circa 1930.

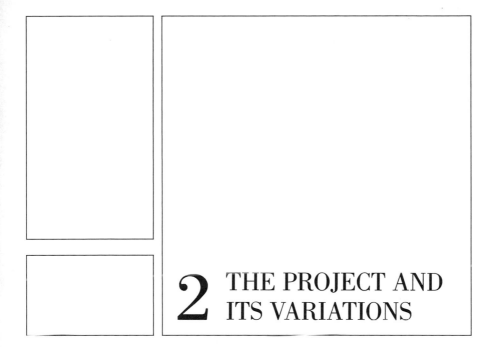

2 THE PROJECT AND ITS VARIATIONS

■ The brief presented to Le Corbusier and Pierre Jeanneret by the Salvation Army for a Cité de Refuge, contained such a range and diversity of functions as to constitute in reality a veritable city unto itself. As a building-type, the Cité de Refuge has precursors in eighteenth- and nineteenth-century charitable institutions, such as foyers for the poor, mariners' hostels, and the not-so-charitable establishments such as the English workhouses, lazarets (quarantine stations), and prisons. However, if these offer certain similarities from an architectural point of view, there are also analogies to be found in the physical spaces planned and in some cases constructed by utopian socialist communities—for example, the Familistère of J.-B. Godin in Guise.

Typological Precedents

Temporary lodgings, or asylums for itinerant workers, vagabonds, or refugees are an ancient institution, primarily but not necessarily situated in urban settings: caravansaries and monasteries served the purpose over time, but it was particularly during the growth of large industrial and commercial cities that dormitory-hotels for individuals (of both sexes) without resources emerged as a specific type. The Albergo dei Poveri in Naples by the architect F. Fuga, which attracted the attention of young Henri Labrouste, is a marvelous example of such an institution. Three contiguous square pavilions, each with an

15

interior courtyard, form a rectangular building; the central square has an axial space with radiating wings, where the refectories and other collective services of the hostel are grouped.

Henry Roberts, who published his famous survey, *Dwellings of the Laboring Classes*, in 1850, mentions another "Albergo dei Poveri" in Naples, unfinished when he visited it in 1829: "One of the most imposing edifices inhabited by the working classes is the Hostel for the Poor . . . ; it already contains 2,600 inhabitants. It has six floors, the last of which has workshops where individuals of different ages and sex are engaged in weaving, in making shoes and clothing, or in working with coral."[1] Roberts also gives examples (with plans dating from 1835) of another kind of establishment, the refuge for needy sailors in England, which is undoubtedly a direct precursor of the Shelters envisaged by General Booth, although they possessed no workshops as the *albergi* did.[2] As an architectural building-type, both of our examples illustrate the basic arrangement of sleeping accommodations in dormitories with numerous beds, the separation of sexes by floor or by wing, and the inclusion of collective eating facilities.

In the late nineteenth century, the municipal authorities of the City of Paris began a program of building public overnight hostels. An architect−civil servant for the city administration drew up the plans for a *refuge de nuit* for men, 107 quai de Valmy, bordering the St. Martin canal.[3] The program itself, and the choice of the location on a major transportation network with heavy barge traffic, and quite near to a railway station, are analogous to that of the Cité de Refuge. An exceptional aspect of this particular hostel is that it is adjacent to, and forms a unit with, a public establishment for disinfection of objects; this feature recalls to mind the parallels between lazarets and overnight shelters for indigents. In the past, the public's desire to isolate the socially ill from society has generally corresponded to the desire to isolate the physically ill in hospitals and lazarets.[4] The Salvation Army did much to combat and to reduce this negative attitude by aiding people where they tended to congregate, namely *within* the city limits.

Although research into the typological sources for the Cité de Refuge reveals a great deal about the nature of the institution, this is not our major concern here; rather, we are interested in discovering how and why Le Corbusier came to conceive this particular formal solution.

The specific requirements of this program, which foresaw the integration of living facilities, social aid, and places of work, provided the direct prototype in architectural terms of Le Corbusier's idea for the Unité d'Habitation of Marseille during post−World War II reconstruc-

tion period in France. But what makes the project for the Cité de Refuge all the more fascinating is the way in which it was profoundly
influenced by—one could even say "conditioned" by—the real constraints of a difficult site and by its insertion into the existing urban
fabric of Paris. What emerges from the archival material is Le Corbusier's effort to transform an existing building-type into a generaliz-
able model which in turn could be used to modify the urban morphology of the neighborhood. This latter point is clearly apparent
in his 1932 project to extend the Cité de Refuge (then under construction) into a vaster complex, a Cité d'Hébergement, on adjoining land.[5]

As previously mentioned, we are interested in the Cité de Refuge
both as a building which is the product of a particular social and political system, and as the expression of the intellectual and aesthetic
concerns of those who designed it. All of this was conditioned by the
economic situation prevailing in France at the time of its creation.

Finances and the Choice of an Architect

The Salvation Army depended upon the donations of philanthropi-
cally inspired individuals, in order to carry out the vast social campaigns and building programs formulated for post–World War I France
by Commissioner Peyron. Unlike the achievement of the Home for
Women in Paris, which was established in an existing building, acquired and then renovated, the Cité de Refuge, the Home for Young
Men, and the project of a shelter for exprisoners of the Bagne de Cayenne (a prison in South America) were to be new constructions.[6] A
fund-raising campaign was launched by the Army to finance these
projects, which lasted from 1929 until 1934, and which included at
least 20,000 contributors for the Cité de Refuge alone. An honorary
committee of patrons was established which included the foremost
politicians and public officials of the time, ambassadors and leaders
of the business community (Catholic, Jewish, Protestant, and nonsec-
tarian). A donation of 500,000 francs initiated the drive, but it was
the gift of 1,800,000 francs by the Princess Edmund de Polignac, decided at a business luncheon with Commissioner Peyron and an under-
secretary of the Ministry of Labor and Hygiene, that permitted the
Army to seek an architect immediately and begin plans.[7]

The Princess de Polignac, born Winaretta Singer (of sewing-machine
fame), is thus a key figure in the affair from the outset, not only because she had already funded the annex to the Palais du Peuple and
ultimately contributed 3 million rather than the 1.8 million francs

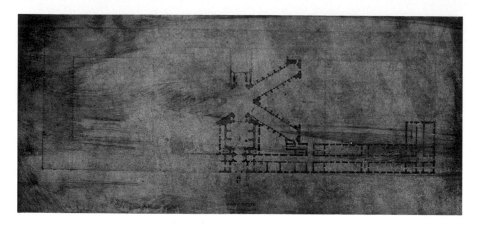

7. Plan, Albergo dei poveri (poorhouse) in Naples, drawn by Henri Labrouste in the nineteenth century.

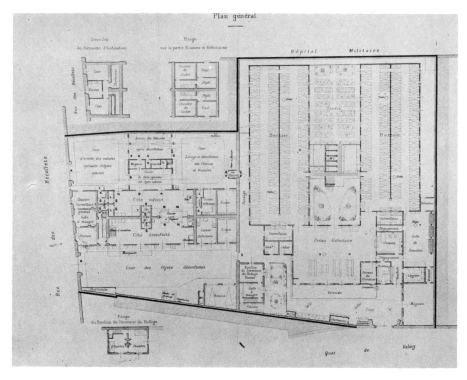

8. Plan, overnight hostel for men at 107 quai de Valmy, Paris. Bouvard architect, 1890. Archives de la Seine.

9. Illustration taken from a fund-raising brochure for the Cité de Refuge by Labarthe.

10. The Princess Winaretta Singer-Polignac.

originally bequeathed to the Cité, but also because as "godmother" to the project, she had a word on the choice of the architect. How Le Corbusier came to the elderly widow's attention remains uncertain; however, a plausible hypothesis is suggested in the following account of her life:

His (Edmund's) wife was the greatest patron of the arts up until the war of 1939. Gabriel Fauré and Stravinsky, Ravel and Igor Markevitch, Debussy and Poulenc, all the great composers of half a century dedicated works to her, which were played in her salons, and all the best musicians were heard at her home. . . .[8]

It is entirely likely that Le Corbusier, an avid concert-goer, accompanied his composer-brother Albert Jeanneret, who moved in the above-mentioned circle of composers, to these *soirées musicales* and thereby made her acquaintance. Le Corbusier designed a house for the Polignacs in 1926, but it was never built. In any event, it was she who more or less imposed her choice of an architect upon the Salvation Army for the design of the annex to the Palais, rue des Cordeliers, in 1926 and the Cité de Refuge.

Le Corbusier was not totally unknown to the Salvation Army at the time, for besides the Palais du Peuple annex, he was also installing dormitory facilities in a barge of reinforced cement, the *Louise Catherine*, for the same client. Moreover, we know that he studied still another project for the Salvation Army, a Maison du Libéré for recently released prisoners of the *bagne* in Cayenne. The frequently stormy collaboration between the architect and the Army went on until 1952.

The client, perhaps somewhat frightened by Le Corbusier's lack of credentials in terms of large-scale completed buildings in 1929, would have preferred to organize a limited competition for the Cité de Refuge before actually choosing an architect, but Le Corbusier, already associated with his cousin Pierre Jeanneret, refused. Thus he obtained his commission.

Following their policy of strategically locating their establishments near to major transportation networks so as to be immediately accessible to their clientele, the Salvation Army sought and obtained the lease of two adjoining plots of land from the City of Paris, situated between the streets of Cantagrel and Chevaleret, at the far limit of the thirteenth *arrondissement* but facing the railroad tracks leading to the Austerlitz-Orléans station.

Only one of the lots (marked "second lot" on the plan) was available at the time that Le Corbusier and Commissioner Peyron had their initial meeting in May 1929. A month after the first project was pre-

11. Le Corbusier, Palais du Peuple extension, rue des Cordeliers, 1926.

12. Interior of a dormitory in the Palais du Peuple.

13. Perspective of the transformed barge *Louise Catherine*.

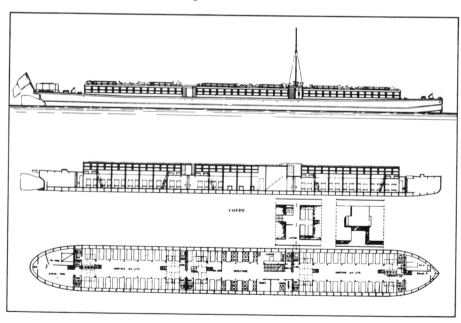

14. Plan, section, facade of the barge-hostel (from L. Corbusier and P. Jeanneret, *l'Oeuvre Complete*, vol. 1 [Zurich, Editions Girsberger, 1930], p. 32).

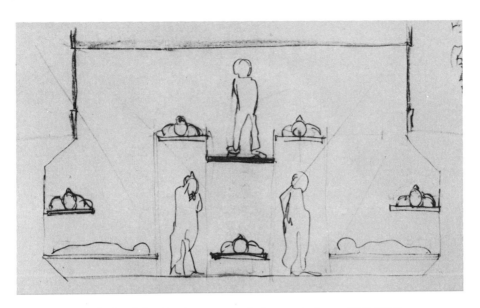

15. Section, study sketch for sleeping accommodations on the barge. FLC 12069.

16. Barge-hostel *Louise Catherine* installed by Le Corbusier for the Salvation Army, Paris 1929–30.

17. Swiss Pavilion, dormitory in Paris, by Le Corbusier, 1930–32.

20. Narkomfin collective housing, Moscow, by M. Ginsburg, 1929–30.

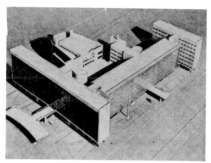

18. Centrosoyus office building, Moscow, by Le Corbusier and N. Kolli, 1928–33.

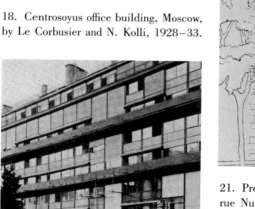

19. Clarté apartment building, Geneva, by Le Corbusier, 1929–32.

21. Preliminary study, apartment building on rue Nungesser et coli, Paris, by Le Corbusier, 1931–33.

sented (June 1929) the city council voted to cede the second lot and demolish the several temporary constructions that existed, thereby providing the Army and their architects with a highly irregular parcel of land of approximately 1,700 square meters.[9]

Conception of the Project

The program which the Salvation Army gave to the architects contained essentially three kinds of services: shelter for sleeping, kitchen and restaurant for the preparing and serving of meals, and workshops for the "rehabilitation" of the labor force. In additions to these, there were to be a number of social and administrative services: meeting hall, lounges for residents, medical consultation rooms, laundry, clothing exchange, offices and lodgings for the personnel. The building was to provide five to six hundred beds, distributed in dormitories and in "roomettes"—intended mainly for single women with babies. Since it was essential, not to say mandatory, from the Army's point of view, that these women work during the day, a crèche was also projected within the establishment. It should be clear, therefore, that the Cité de Refuge was destined to be *more* than simply a shelter for the night, but would have facilities at various levels which functioned throughout the day, catering to the widest possible variety of human needs.

The internal relationships between these facilities, as well as their accessibility from outside, provided a very complex and sensitive task for Pierre Jeanneret and Le Corbusier. There was the principal problem of filtering and distributing people according to diverse criteria of age, sex, need, and qualification.

In order to understand the great significance of this building, one must bear in mind the key ideas which determined its form from the very beginning: first, that it should be an airtight envelope, with a fixed, glazed curtain-wall suspended on the south facade of the main dormitory building, and second, that it should provide for the artificial control of the interior environment, that is, the mechanical supply of heated, purified air. The conception of the building itself is more "revolutionary" from an aesthetic and technological standpoint than it is from a social and political one: the economic justifications and the biological implications that he advanced in favor of this technical solution were more controversial and disturbing to conventional ideas than the fact that it went against existing legal codes or bourgeois social preconceptions. The Cité forced a new awareness upon public and professionals alike because of the architectural imagery rather than for any social changes it implied in terms of a communitarian residential environment. Lastly, the Cité de Refuge in its final form set forth a model for the gradual restructuring, through incremental steps, of the entire surrounding urban tissue of the neighborhood. Its evolution from the first preliminary project to the final completed edifice illustrates how this idea progressed from what initially was merely an attempt to fit the programmed building onto the site to a resolution with much greater impact. Shortly after the building's completion, Le Corbusier was to claim that the manner by which the problem of dwelling was stated and subsequently resolved at the Cité de Refuge constituted the fundamental basis of a modern architecture and urban planning.

Design Phases

Four and one-half years is a long time for a building to be in the process of design and construction; nonetheless, between June 1929 and June 1930 when the cornerstone was laid, the Cité de Refuge passed through five preliminary versions, and the definitive plans were continually redesigned during the construction, which lasted until December 1933. This was not, it should be noted, the *end* of the process, for the building was then modified against Le Corbusier's wishes but nevertheless under both architects' supervision, from 1934 until the early 1950s.

Of special interest to us is the fact that during this first period of the Cité's conception and birth, three other important projects by the same architects were under way, works which contain numerous points of comparison with the Cité: the Clarté apartment house in Geneva, the Swiss dormitory in Paris, and Le Corbusier's own apartment building, 24 rue Nungesser et Coli. Finally, potentially just as significant as the architect's own internal development, as can be perceived through the design of these buildings, was the fact that he visited the Soviet Union on several occasions (1928, 1929), and his visits brought him in contact with the experimental collective housing projects being built by Moses Ginsburg. The achievement of the Narkomfin (1928–30) in Moscow most certainly held lessons for Le Corbusier precisely at the moment he was designing the Cité de Refuge—while also attempting to convince the Soviets to construct his Centrosoyus office building.[10]

Initial designs (Projects 1–4) were greatly conditioned by two important constraints: (*a*) the shape and the availability of the terrain in two stages; and (*b*) the existence of strictly enforced codes on building heights within the boundaries of Paris. Thus, the *parti* selected in

Project 1: June–July 1929

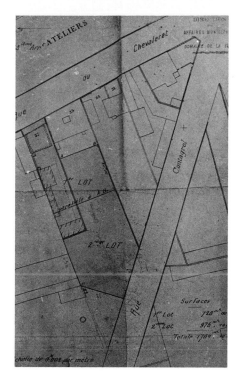

22. Plan of lots including the future site of the Cité de Refuge in the thirteenth *arrondissement*, Paris, 1929.

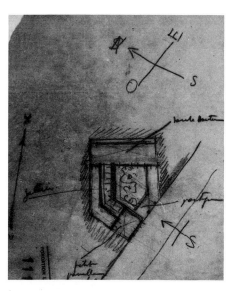

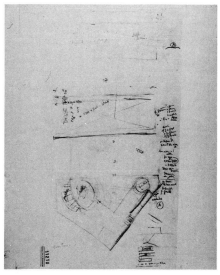

23. Sketch plan, Project 1 (May–June, 1929), using available half of the site on the rue Cantagrel. FLC 1119.

24. Sketch plan, entrance level on rue Cantagrel, Project 1. FLC 11210.

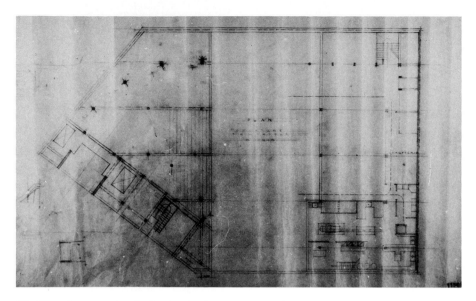

25. Plan, basement level, showing kitchens, stairs, and structural system. Project 1. 12 June 1929. FLC 11506.

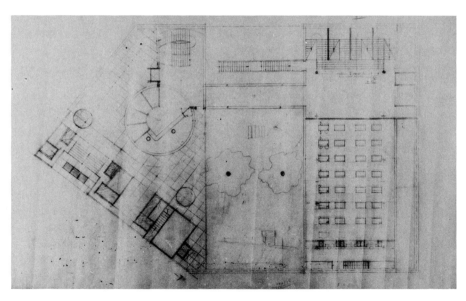

26. Plan, entrance level (ground floor), with reception area, pavilion, bridge, restaurant, and stairs to garden below grade. Project 1. FLC 11516.

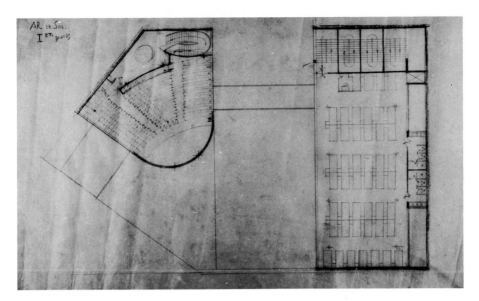

27. Plan, first floor. Conference hall above the reception area, dormitories in main building. Project 1. 17 June 1929. FLC 11521.

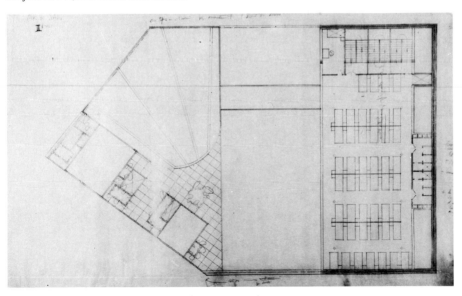

28. Plan, second floor. Dormitories. Project 1. FLC 11494.

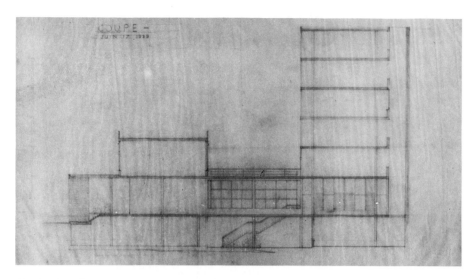

29. Section, Project 1. 12 June 1929. FLC 11515.

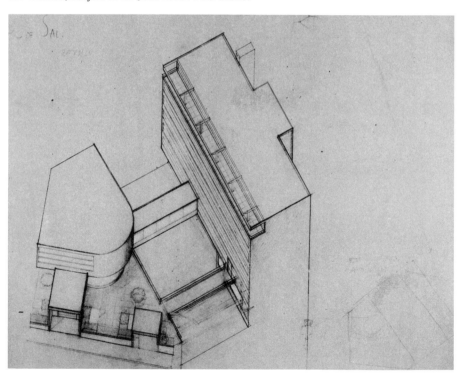

30. Axonometric drawing, Project 1. June 1929. FLC 11222.

Project 2: July–September 1929

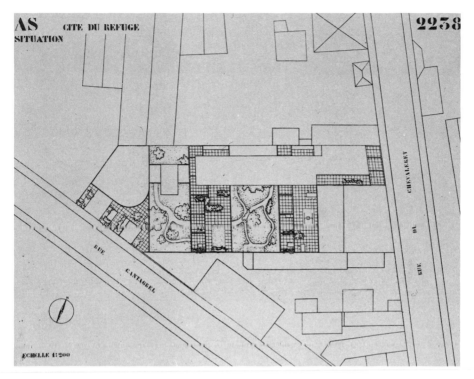

31. Site plan with landscaping for Project 2, no. 2238. FLC 10605.

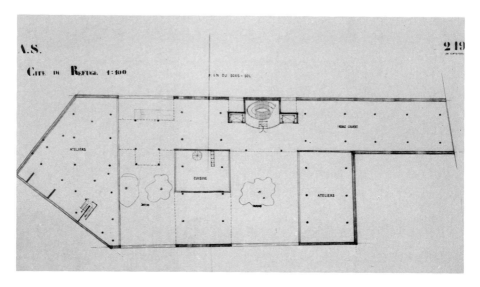

32. Plan, basement/pilotis level, no. 2195. Project 2. September 1929. Workshops are under the entrance platform. FLC 10592.

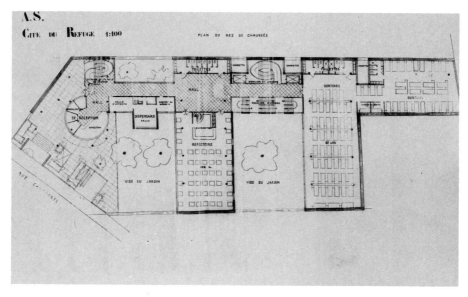

33. Plan, ground floor, no. 2196. Project 2. Reception area, dispensary, restaurant, dormitories. FLC 10594.

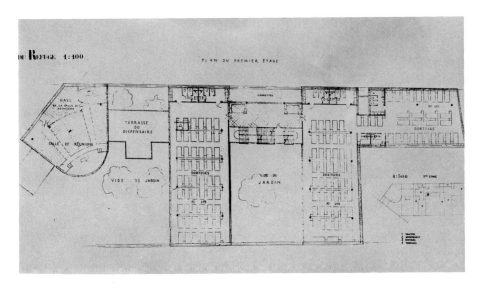

34. Plan of first floor, no. 2197. Project 2. Conference hall and dormitories.

35. Perspective study of reception pavilion, rue Cantagrel, and the high-rise dormitory building. Project 2. FLC 11497.

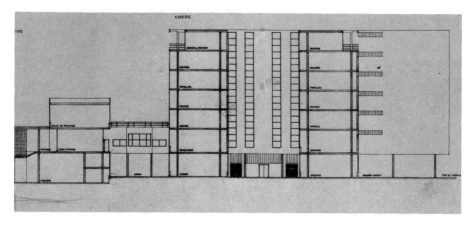

36. Section no. 2199. Project 2. Men's dormitories on two floors, then women, families, sick persons, and children. FLC 10597.

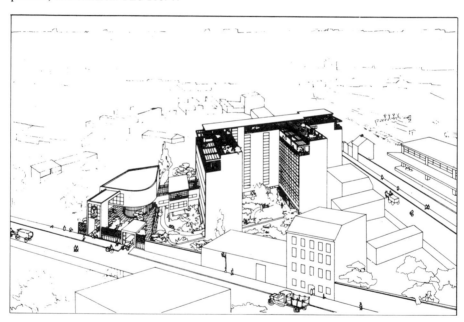

37. Axonometric view, Project 2. (Redrawn by H. Lapprand)

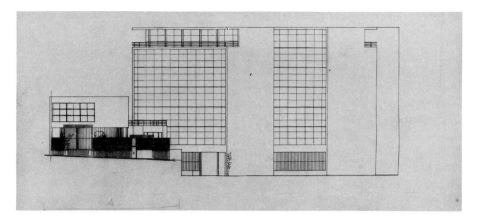

38. Elevation no. 2198. Project 2. FLC 10596.

39. Perspective view from the garden. Project 2.

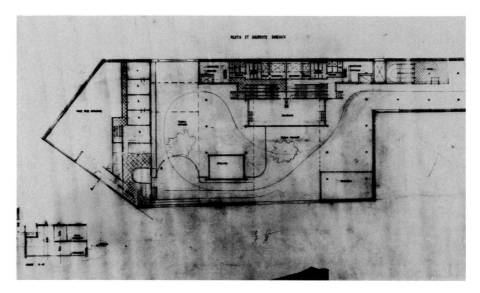

40. Plan, pilotis level. Preparatory study for Project 3. Workshops, kitchen, and offices. FLC 11102.

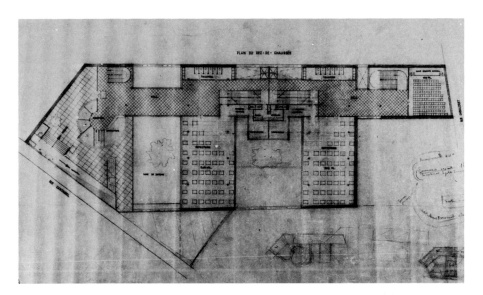

41. Plan, ground floor. Preparatory study for Project 3. Entrance pavilion, halls, restaurants.
Note thumbnail sketches for moving entrance pavilion to a more central location, and separating
the Cité into a western, women's wing and an eastern, men's wing. FLC 11241.

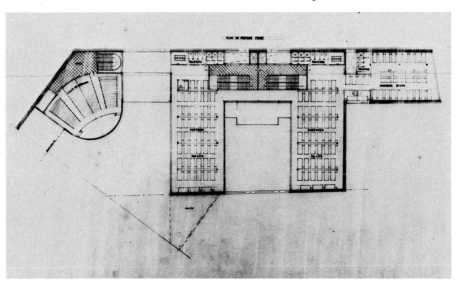

42. Plan, first floor, Preparatory study for Project 3. Dormitories and conference hall. FLC
11088.

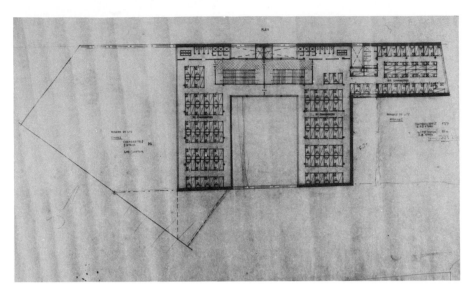

43. Plan, upper floor. Preparatory study for Project 3. Individual sleeping compartments ("boxes") installed in all three wings. FLC 11243.

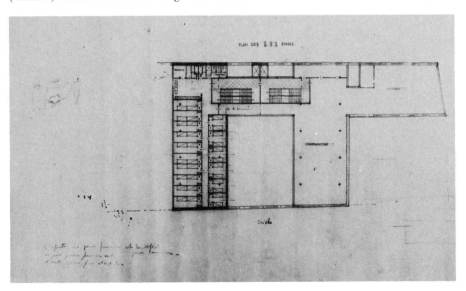

44. Plan, third, fourth, and fifth floors. Preparatory study for Project 3. One- and two-bed roomettes. FLC 11101.

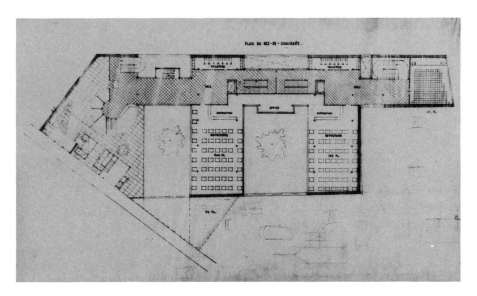

45. Plan, ground floor. Preparatory study for Project 3. September, 1929. Reception pavilion, hall restaurants. FLC 11075.

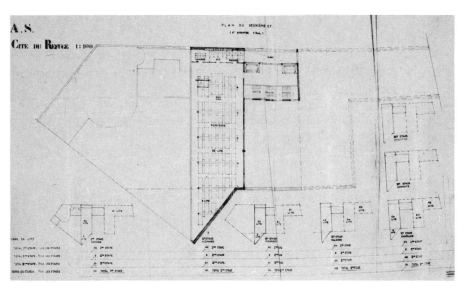

46. Plan, second and upper floors. Preparatory sketch for Project 3. Diagrams illustrating future additions by stages. FLC 11246.

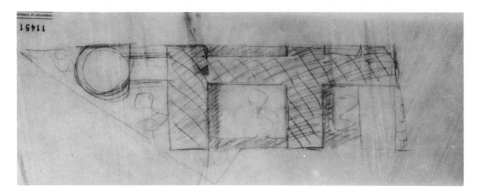

47. Site plan, rough sketch of building which resembles Project 2 except for a rotunda entrance pavilion on the west. FLC 11451.

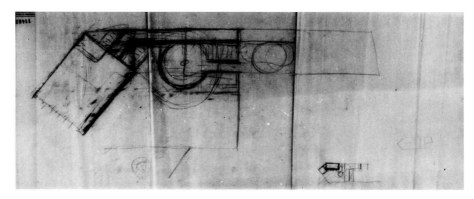

48. Site plan, rough sketch of the rotunda placed between entrance platform on the west and the main building on the east, accessible by bridge(s). FLC 11462.

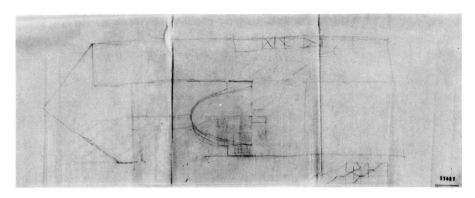

49. Site plan, rough sketch with a hyperbolic rather than circular entrance pavilion contiguous to the northeast dormitory wing. FLC 11461.

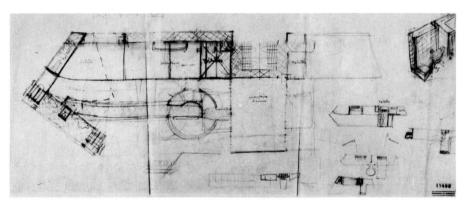

50. Plan and perspective view of alternative solutions. This is a crucial worksheet where the definitive composition of volumes for the Cité first appears. Two parallel axes running east-west along the site. FLC 11468.

Project 1 concerned only the western portion of the total eventual site, that bordering the rue Cantagrel; although the City of Paris had agreed to lease the land to the Salvation Army, the official decision on the adjoining plot, at 37 rue Chevaleret, was not made until July 1929. A sketch indicated the siting of a tall building and a low gallery forming two sides of a square along the eastern and northern limits, which attached to a small entrance pavilion on the rue Cantagrel. Because of the irregular shape of the plot, whose frontage on the rue Cantagrel is oriented at forty-five degrees off the main axis running through to the rue Chevaleret, the problem of the entry provoked numerous attempts to find a suitable solution. Second, as the level of the ground was higher on the rue Cantagrel than on the rue Chevaleret, from the out-set the architects had envisaged a building reposing on free-standing columns and the creation of a garden below grade. This option be-came a permanent feature of all subsequent proposals.

The Four Preliminary Projects

Project 1 for the Cité de Refuge illustrated a characteristic of Le Corbusier's architecture which is rarely noticed or sufficiently appre-ciated, namely that inherent in the structure was the eventuality of reorganization of spaces for extension over time. The first idea for the Cité was a partial solution, while awaiting the availability of the entire plot; a second building would then be added. The problem of en-trances to the building was resolved by creating a wedge-shaped plat-form at the level of the rue Cantagrel. One entered in a conventional fashion, perpendicular to the sidewalk, although the buildings were ranged at an angle to it, and proceeded to a round reception pavilion and waiting room; and there was a separate kiosk on this entrance "quay"[11] which was intended for reception of merchandise. The cir-cular entrance pavilion, surmounted by a parabolically-shaped con-ference hall, was linked to the dormitory building by a bridge-like gallery or "gangway," the transition from street to gallery being subtly accomplished by use of this feature.

Noted on a sketch was the observation that twenty meters was the maximum height allowed for structures bordering on the rue Can-tagrel, and thus it was below this fixed ceiling that the architects con-ceived five floors of dormitories, with men located on the first level, then women, the sick, the children, and finally families. On the street level of the main block were situated the refectory, and below this the kitchen, at garden level. The oblong site running east-west dictated the placing of stairwells along the northern perimeter, in order to permit maximum natural lighting from the south and west for the major activity spaces. However, building codes in Paris forbid the creation of windows in a party wall that is directly adjacent to a neighbor's property line, without his explicit approval; hence, small courts serving as lightwells were created along the northern limit of the Cité in order to bring light from the side into the stairwells, washrooms, and toilets. In Project 1 the garden could also be reached from the hall of the dormitory building by an exterior stairway. A full development of this initial *parti* was drawn up during July and August 1929 (after the second plot became available for construction) and presented to the Salvation Army on 25 September 1929.

Project 2 intended a second dormitory on a north-south axis, parallel to the first, and a third one perpendicular to these two, and abutting onto the rue Chevaleret, the whole forming a kind of "M" in its layout. When compared to the edifice actually built on the site, this second solution (which gave rise to numerous perspective views) presented a rather modest image, thoughtfully integrated into the existing urban tissue of Paris, in spite of its radically modernist aesthetic. One might even venture to call it a peculiarly "Parisian" solution, with interior court formed by two wings that terminate in blind party walls, as do so many of the nineteenth-century buildings in the French capital. The perpendicular north-south wings were justified in part by the necessity for maintaining the structure within the height limitations, while providing a maximum of usable surface. Only the western facade of each wing had a glazed curtain-wall, the eastern facades having small windows (as in the Swiss dormitory), or none at all. For a formal standpoint, Project 2 had a great deal more in common with the architectural aspect of Le Corbusier's villas of the late 1920s (Plainex, Church, and those in Stuttgart), his project for the Draeger publishing house in Paris, or with the Centrosoyus in Moscow, than it had with the more sculptural oeuvre of the early 1930s, notably the Swiss Dormitory and buildings for Algiers. In fact, throughout these preliminary projects for the Cité de Refuge, we may discern this very change in vocabulary, also reflected in the figurative elements of his paintings of 1929–30.

Weaknesses in the architectural conception of these early proposals are clearly evident in the handling of the circulation of persons and goods, and of the interior arrangement of sleeping spaces. The pilotis (or columns upon which the building sits) obstructed the easy circulation of trucks serving the kitchen and workshops from the rue Chevaleret. These levels were all accessible to adjacent stairways, although it would appear to be a strange decision to place the sick ward between a floor for children above and for women below. Moreover, somewhat tortuous stairs were proposed for linking the main entrance hall to the conference hall, and for reaching the ground floor from the garden. More expedient solutions were found finally, which avoided the indiscriminate mixing of all ages and sexes, particularly on the main stairs.

Sleeping arrangements in the dormitory spaces of Project 1 consisted of double rows of six beds placed within an area delimited by columns, the double row separated by a partition. With Project 2 the partition was aligned on the axis between pairs of columns, increasing the number of beds which could be fitted into the spaces. However, when it was a matter of creating individual cells, each with a bed, desk, and cupboard, the number of beds in a row was necessarily reduced (to four), and the dividing partition was again moved off-axis.

The difficulty of fitting the required *number* of beds into the dormitories was at least temporarily resolved in Project 3, when a curious proposal was made by Le Corbusier to acquire and build upon a triangular piece of land, adjacent to the actual site and touching upon the rue Cantagrel. The purpose, according the Le Corbusier, in trying to secure this additional piece of land was to protect the view from the Cité de Refuge against any future developer who might erect a tall edifice that would obstruct the natural lighting and visibility on the south. At this point, perhaps because of difficulties in the Salvation Army's fund-raising campaign for the Cité, the architects had proposed construction of the entire complex in three stages: the western wing first, followed by the triangular extension and, finally, the other two wings on the east. A fifth and sixth floor were also added to the building. The total number of beds would thereby have been raised from the 500 initially foreseen to 680.

Significant and critical changes in the project occurred in April 1930, following Le Corbusier's return from a trip to Moscow. The Princess de Polignac had made a further donation of funds so that the Cité might be accomplished in a single operation. A series of rough sketches, the first of a ground floor plan for Project 3, illustrates graphically the architect's creative effort to incorporate the dormitory facilities into a single, more unified and frontal volume, with the entrance and social services forming a series of low buildings strung out before a high-rise volume. One of the north-south wings was eliminated altogether, after an initial attempt to place the rotunda between the two wings; the rotunda was then imagined first to the south of, and then tangential to, the gallery connecting the entrance kiosk and the remaining high-rise wing; then the rotunda was momentarily aban-

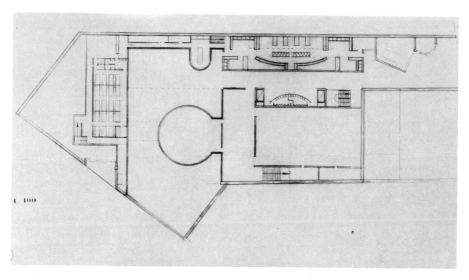

51. Plan, pilotis and garden, no. 2381, Project 4. Kitchen, toilets, conference hall(?), and dormitories for the elderly. FLC 10608.

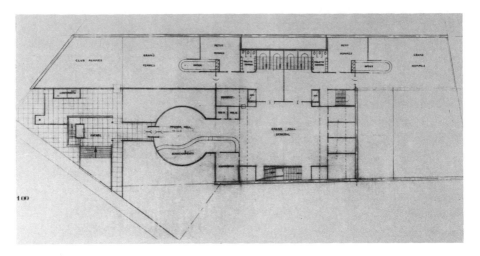

52. Plan, ground floor, no. AS 2380, Project 4. Entrance pavilion, first hall, large hall, small and large dining rooms for men and for women, and a club-lounge for women. FLC 10606.

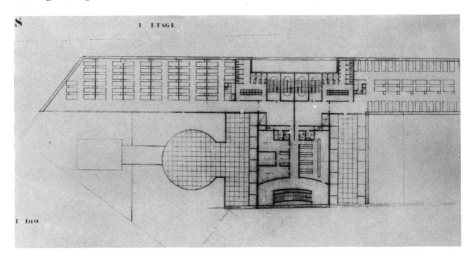

53. Plan no. AS 2382, first floor, Project 4. Dormitories for men and for women, infirmary, and clothing exchange. FLC 10610.

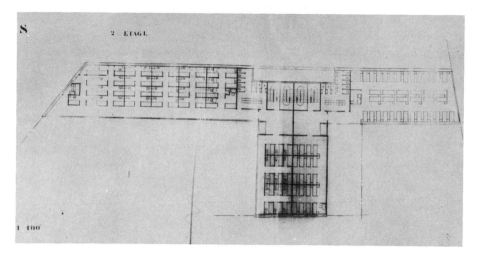

54. Plan no. AS 2383, second floor, Project 4. Dormitories for men and for women. FLC 10611.

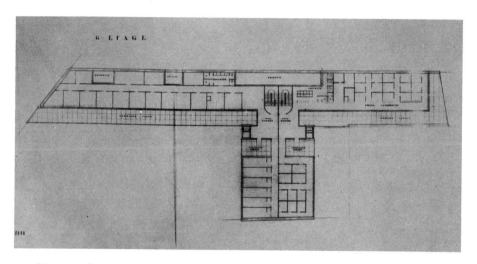

55. Plan no. AS 2385, sixth floor, Project 4. Roomettes for men and for women, terraces. FLC 10601.

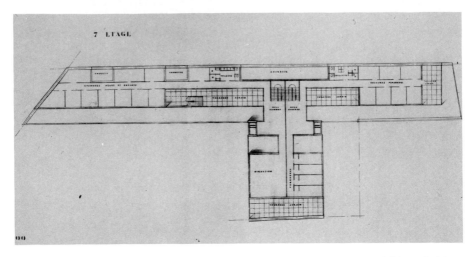

56. Plan no. AS 2386, seventh floor, Project 4. Roomettes for women with children, lodgings for the director and personnel. FLC 10602.

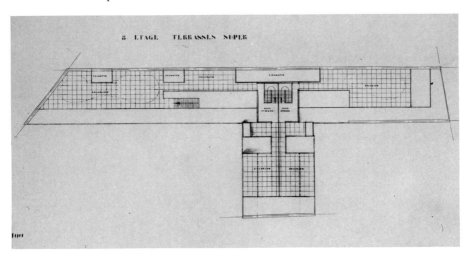

57. Plan no. AS 2387, eighth floor, Project 4. Solaria. FLC 10603.

58. Elevation, Project 4 (circa 30 April 1930). Ink sketch by Le Corbusier showing entrance pavilion, covered bridge, and rotunda attached to a single wing perpendicular to and rising to the full height of the dormitory building. FLC 11179.

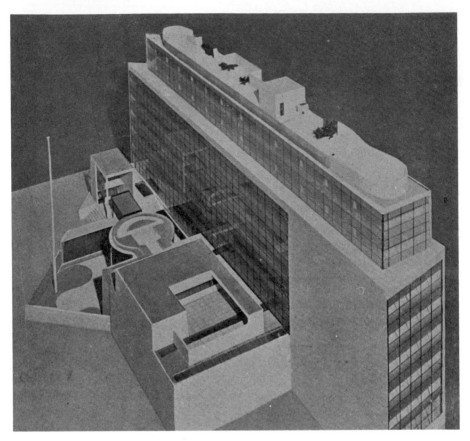

59. Model by Maquettes PERFECTA, Paris, of Project 5 for the Cité de Refuge. (From *L'Architecture d'Aujourd'hui* 2, December 1930, p. 17)

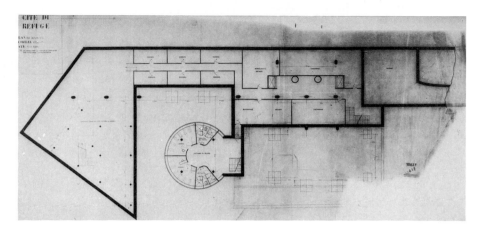

60. Plan no. CR 2412, basement Project 5. Storerooms, workshops, etc. FLC 10627.

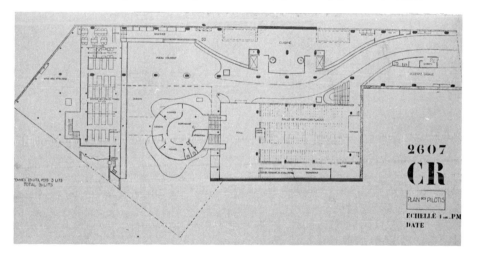

61. Plan, pilotis level, no. CR 2607, with dormitory for the elderly, dispensary, conference hall, kitchen, and passage to rue du Chevaleret.

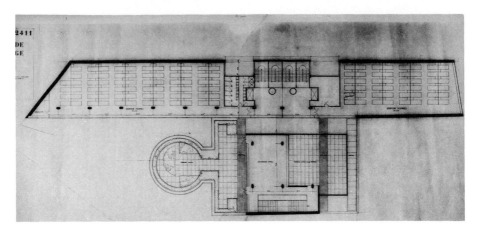

62. Plan no. CR 2411, first floor, Project 5. FLC 10625, 1 and 2.

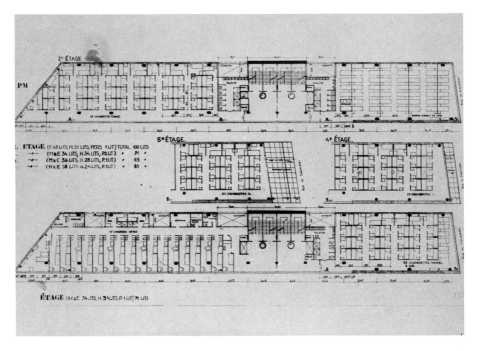

63. Plans of the second, third, fourth, and fifth floors, showing the dormitories for women with "boxes," dormitories for men with and without "boxes," and chambrettes for women on the fifth floor. FLC 10705.

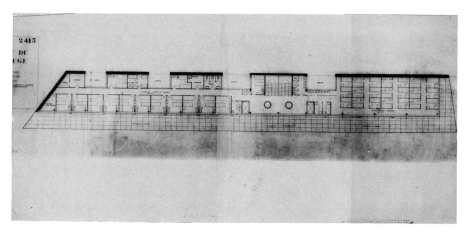

64. Plan no. CR 2415, sixth floor, Project 5. Bedrooms with two beds for women and children and chambrettes for men. FLC 10636.

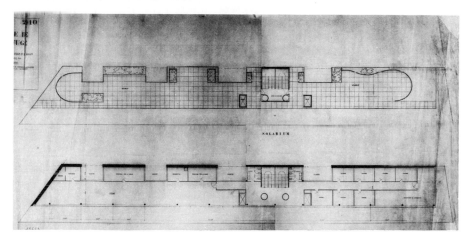

65. Plan no. CR 2410, seventh and eighth floors, Project 5. Crèche and apartments for personnel and the director. FLC 10623.

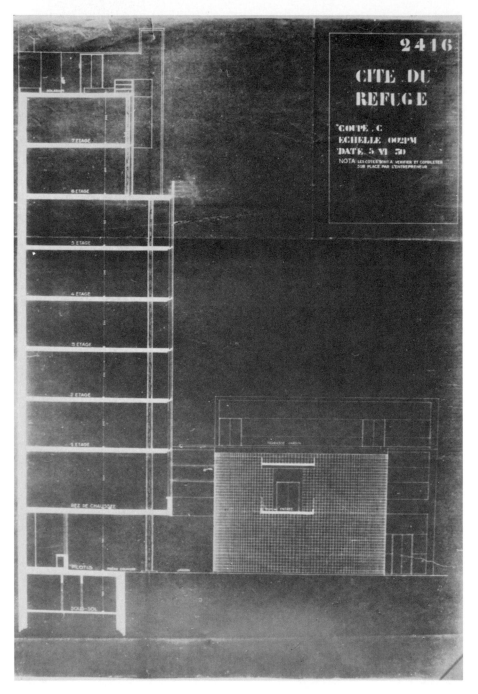

66. Section no. CR 2416, Project 5, 5 June 1930. Blueprint of transversal section through the dormitory building and entrance bridge. Note that the glass curtain-wall is absolutely vertical and that an exterior stairway links the seventh floor crèche to the roof terrace. FLC 10640.

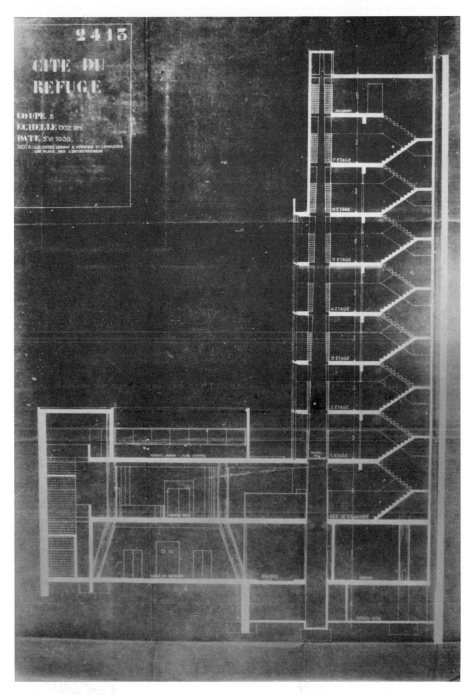

67. Section, no. CR 2413, Project 5, 5 June 1930. Blueprint of section through main hall, conference hall on lower level, and dormitory building. One of a series of plans submitted for a building permit. FLC 10630.

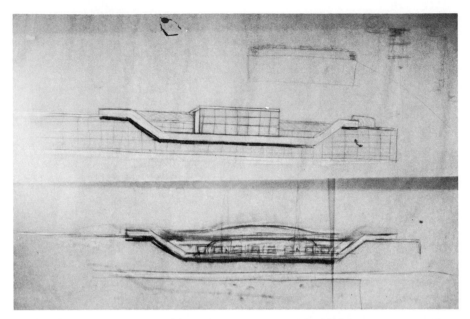

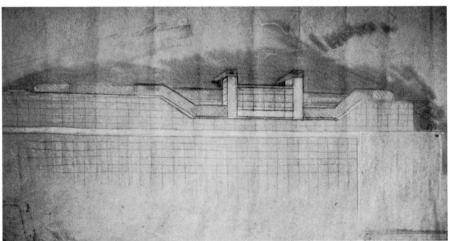

68, 69. Elevations of the south facade. Detail studies of upper floors with variations for exterior stairs from the crèche to the solarium.

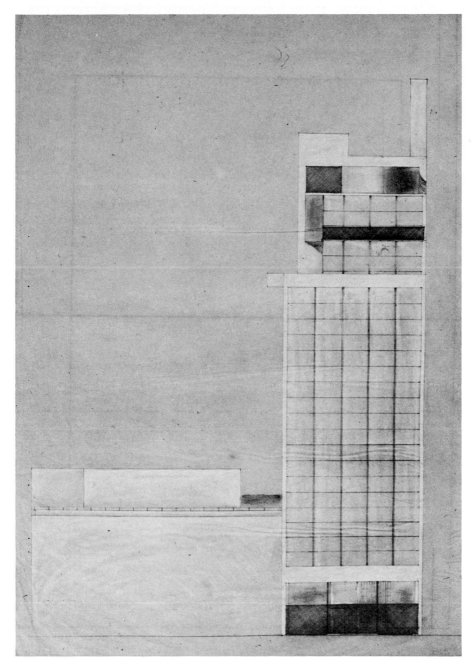

70. Elevation sketch in colored chalk for east facade, rue du Chevaleret, Project 5.

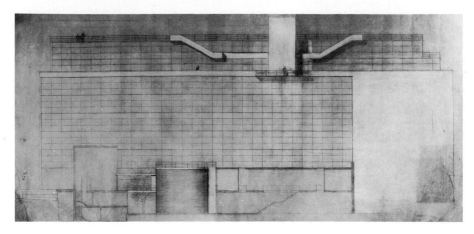

71. Elevation study of south facade with sections of lower buildings. FLC 11115.

72. Model showing the definitive solution for the south facade, Project 5. Note that there are no longer exterior stairs.

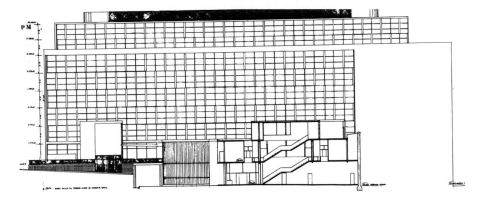

73. Elevation of the south facade in the definitive project, with sections through the entrance pavilion and social services building.

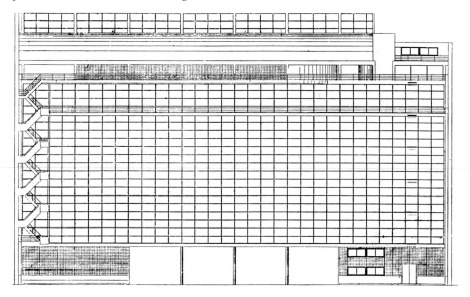

74. Project for a facade dated July 1928 done for the Draeger printing company. Note the similarities with the Cité. (From *l'Oeuvre Complete.*)

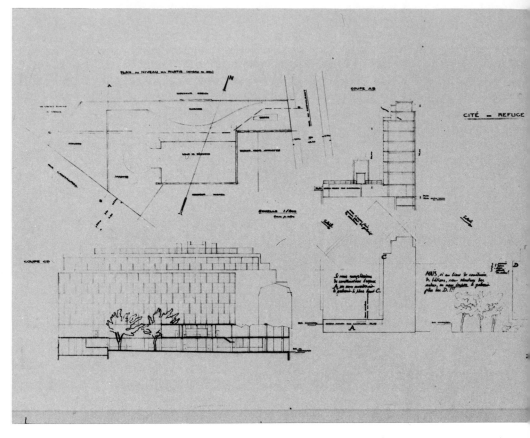

75. Document drawn up by Pierre Jeanneret and Le Corbusier for the Prefecture de la Seine to show how, in their opinion, the building height regulations should be applied to their Project 5 for the Cité de Refuge. In the case that the area (marked "A") below grade on the rue Cantagrel were built upon right to the street level, then the code would allow a maximum height "C"; since the architects on the contrary intended to plant this space with trees and shrubbery, the maximum height would be brought down to "D." For this reason the architects felt their project was being penalised, and added a polemical comment: "Punished for having planted trees!" FLC 11105.

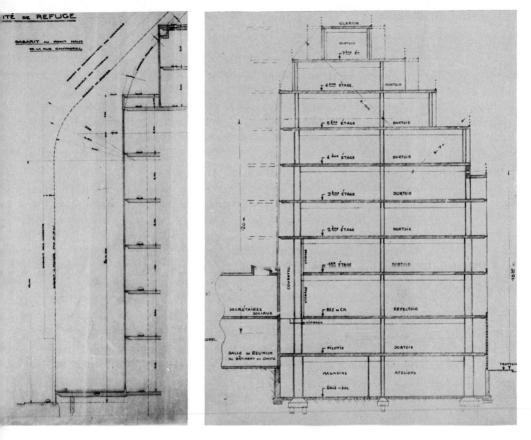

76. Section of the Cité de Refuge, Project 5, illustrating the way of calculating the maximum legal height for a building on the rue Cantagrel. This project was refused a building permit because portions of the sixth and eighth floors extended forty centimeters beyond the accepted limit. FLC 11226.

77. Section no. CR 2732. Note the slight inclining of the southern facade adopted so that the building would not exceed the height limitation. FLC 10802.

Cité d'Hébergement, City for Wayfarers: June–September 1932

The commission to design a Cité d'Hébergement, projected as an extension to the Cité de Refuge, involved 56,665 cubic meters of temporary lodgings for 300 poor and homeless families (approximately 1,500 persons). As mentioned at the beginning of chapter 2, this project offered Le Corbusier his first concrete opportunity to test the relevance of his model for a Radiant City of the future on a real site. Instead of being a theoretical project located on a perfectly flat landscape, the Cité d'Hébergement was to have buildings placed on the rather steeply sloping terrain between Cantagrel and Chevaleret streets. Le Corbusier took advantage of the topography by using galleries and ramps to link the seven buildings to one another as well as to the Cité de Refuge, which was already under construction at the time. Automobile and pedestrian movement within the complex are completely separate; spaces between buildings, which are on columns, have been planted with trees and treated as green spaces. This proposal for urban restructuring on a neighborhood scale coincides in time with Le Corbusier's first designs for Algiers but antedates those for Antwerp, Belgium, and for the Bastion Kellerman and Ilot 6 in Paris.

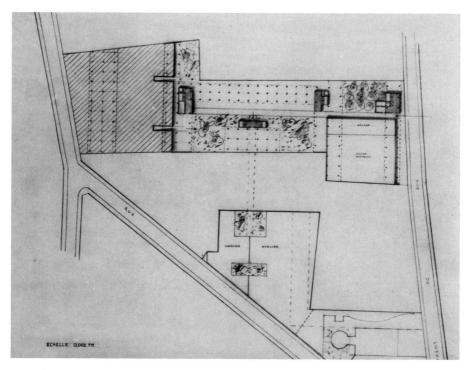

78. Plan of pilotis level, Cité d'Hébergement project, showing workshops, kitchen, and furniture storage. FLC 11017.

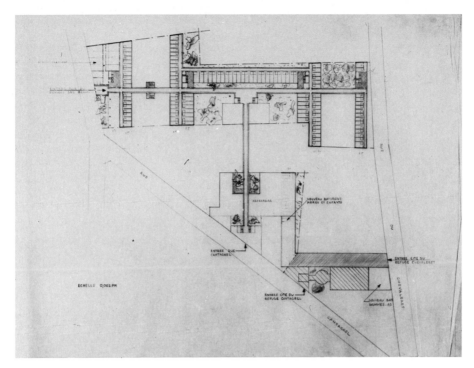

79. Plan, Cité d'Hébergement projected between the rue du Chevaleret and the rue du Dessous des Berges. New building for mothers and children, refectory, rooms for single and married persons with children, administrative wing. Note also a much smaller projected extension of the men's wing of the Cité de Refuge, adjacent to the entry on the rue du Chevaleret. Neither was executed. September 1932. FLC 11043.

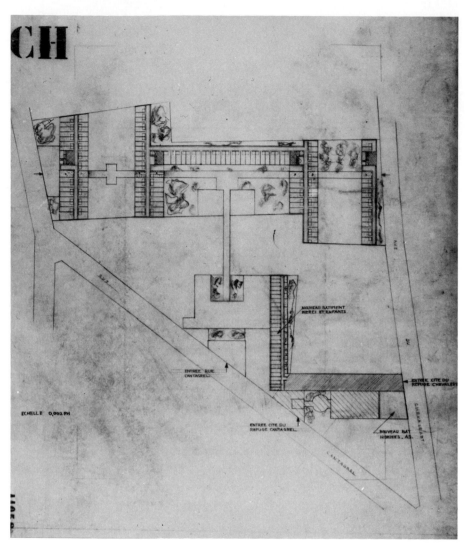

80. Plan of a typical floor with rooms for families, new building for mothers with children and one for men. FLC 11058.

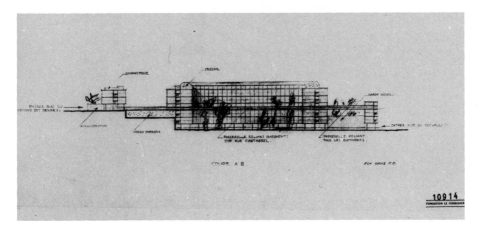

81. Section, Cité d'Hébergement, showing the integration of the building to a hilly terrain. There is a grand concourse running east-west through the building, which includes cooperatives, libraries, gymnasia, crèches, dispensaries, etc. Note that this structure was designed at the same moment as the *batiment-pont* (building-as-bridge) for Algiers proposed by Le Corbusier. September 1932. FLC 10914.

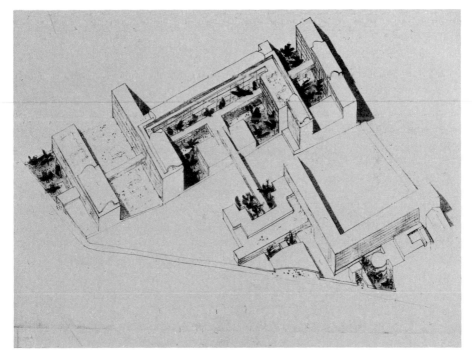

82. Axonometric view of the proposed Cité d'Hébergement, a vast addition to the Cité de Refuge then under construction. Destined for unemployed workers, political refugees, etc. September 1932. FLC 10910.

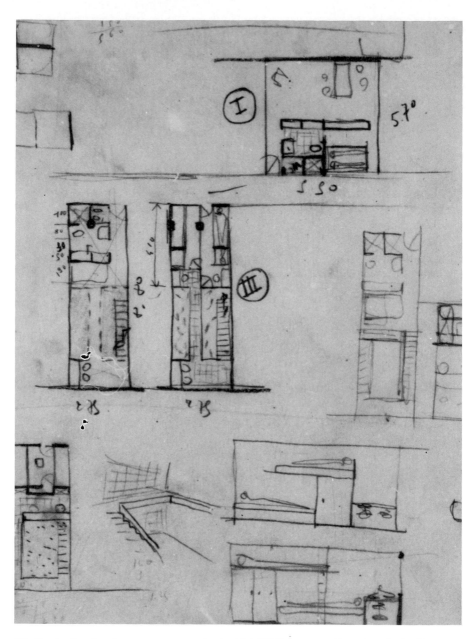

83. Study sketches for apartment-types in the Cité d'Hébergement. Note the split-level spaces, with bridge connecting upper-level sleeping areas. This idea appears in studies for the "Clarte" in Geneva, and apartments in Oued Ouchaia, Algeria. FLC 28222.

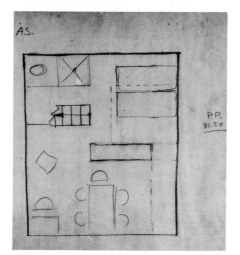
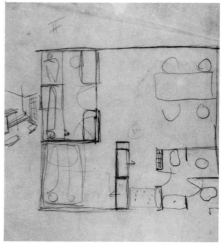

84. Study sketch, plan for an apartment type in the future Cité d'Hébergement. FLC 28189.
85. Plan, first level of a duplex unit with 81.5 cubic meters. FLC 11260.

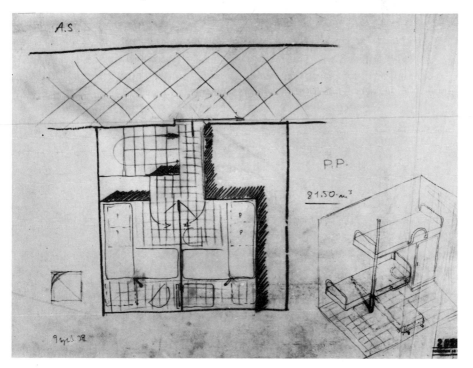

86. Plan, second level and perspective of one-half of sleeping arrangement for six persons in this apartment-type. FLC 28209.

doned in favor of a pavilion, parabolic in shape, with a bridge to the entrance quay. The definitive solution became apparent in a series of sketches that were the basis of Project 4: a seven-story building occupying nearly the full length of the site, with one perpendicular wing on the south. The rotunda was then moved along the main axis of the building to a position close to the southern wing, and it was linked to the street entrance by a bridge. A perspective sketch on this same sheet represented a scheme with other radiating bridges leading into the building like spokes from a wheel.

The principal concerns for the architect at this critical stage in the project must certainly have been as much economic in nature as they were aesthetic: construction, heating, and maintenance costs were reduced through a compression of dispersed spaces into a more unified volume. Project 4, the plans for which date from April 1930, differed from Project 5 of two months later, only in that the idea of a perpendicular wing as high as the rest of the building has still been retained as feasible. Otherwise, the new disposition of functions, which was now defined, included the entrance, rotunda, and large hall, around which the offices were arranged; below this hall at garden level was the conference hall; also located at the garden level were the kitchen, and a small dormitory for the elderly, just beneath the entrance platform. On the ground floor were restaurants and a lounge ("club") for women to the west, and two restaurants for men to the east; this clear separation of services for different sexes was continued on the upper floors, accessible by adjacent but noncommunicating sets of stairs. The first floor provided dormitories for men and women, infirmary, pharmacy, clothing exchange, and terraces; on the second floor, dormitories for men but private rooms (or "boxes" as they are sometimes referred to in French) for women. A setback was introduced on the eastern and southern facades at the sixth-floor level, where terraces were created outside the dormitories and rooms for mothers with children; this also proved necessary for the seventh floor, where apartments for personnel and the Director were located. The eighth floor was entirely devoted to solaria. Numerous studies were made for the elevations of this project, on rue Cantagrel and Chevaleret, taking into consideration the height restrictions and the form of the curtainwall, which covered two-thirds of the southern and portions of the eastern facades of the high structure.

Definitive Project

The "final" proposal for the Cité de Refuge, Project 5, prepared for the Salvation Army in June 1930, did not foresee the perpendicular wing, although Le Corbusier did still make reference to its eventual construction in a letter of the following October. It appears that the foundations were supposed to be executed in such a way as to permit the addition of six stories at a later date.[12] That this incremental achievement of the building was explicitly anticipated in the planning is a fundamental aspect of Le Corbusier's approach, but in this case he soon decided that to build the wing would ultimately obstruct and disfigure the visual, as well as functional, attributes of the southern facade.

Project 5 served as the basis for a model of the future Cité and for the request for a building permit, after the cornerstone already had been laid on 24 June 1930 by M. Désiré Ferry, Minister of Public Hygiene. The entrance now comprised a low, cubical portico open to the south and east and closed on the other two sides—with a wall of glass bricks on the west and ceramic tiles on the north. A covered bridge led to the circular *plaque tournante* (or distribution center). Partially enclosed with glass bricks that joined the two-story building containing the large hall, offices, men's lounge, terraces, and apartments, to the conference hall, below grade. The infirmary and clothing exchange were located in the lower level of the rotunda. This succession of low buildings, of remarkable geometric purity, had as a backdrop the eleven-level residential building, whose facade was a steel and glass curtain-wall nearly two-thirds of its length from the fourth level (first floor) to the eighth level (fifth floor). A setback was introduced, with another curtain-wall enclosing the ninth and tenth levels. It is interesting to observe the numerous studies for symmetrical exterior stairways on the southern facade, connecting the newly introduced child day-care center (crèche) on the tenth level with the eleventh-level terrace and solarium. These stairs (one of which was actually built and then demolished during construction), the metal balustrades, and the chimneys for heating and ventilation were the elements whose treatment most closely resembled the quality of superstructures in naval architecture.

There is little indication that the architects ever consulted the building codes in force concerning such functions as dormitories, restaurants, day-care centers, and the like at the time the plans were being drawn up; they were, however, obliged to take the height restrictions imposed on buildings in inner Paris into account when their projected facade on the rue Chevaleret measured 27.50 meters to the point of the first setback, instead of the 18.50 meters allowed.[13] The facade rue Cantagrel, which also measured 27.50 meters, although separated from the property line on the street by a garden, nevertheless exceeded the 20-meter limit. In September 1930, therefore, the Association de l'Armée du Salut requested, on behalf of the architects, a tolerance from the General Council on Civil Buildings, the administrative body empowered to grant permission to exceed the legal limits. The legislation establishing the heights of buildings, calculated according to the width of the street in question, was a decree dated 13 August 1902, wherein article 43 states, as Pierre Jeanneret reported,

The Prefect of the Seine may authorize tolerances, following the recommendation of the General Council on Civic Buildings and the approval of the Minister of the Interior, concerning the code on heights of buildings for private constructions with a monumental character or with artistic, scientific, or industrial interest.[14]

After Pierre Jeanneret had discovered this clause, the architects wrote a letter in December 1930 to the *Préfet* of the Seine, without even waiting for the General Council to give its opinion—which they had expected to be unfavorable, since its president was Paul Nenot, an architect whom Le Corbusier had violently attacked in the press over his winning entry in the League of Nations competition of 1927![15] Included in their letter to the *Préfet*, chief administrative officer for Paris, which had no mayor at the time, was a new proposal in which they reduced but did not eliminate altogether the excess height on the rue Chevaleret. One should also recognize in passing that the architects may have erred in publishing their project, with photographs of the model, in the December 1930 issue of *l'Architecture d'Aujourd'hui* magazine, before receiving the desired authorization. Their strategy of private, behind-the-scenes maneuvering and outspoken polemics in fact probably backfired on them.

As anticipated, when the General Council considered the request for a tolerance at its meeting in January 1931, it refused to sanction an increase in the elevation even to the absolute maximum of 20 meters on the rue Chevaleret, observing that:

—Considering that the Commission on Streets believes that the needs of the National Railway Company will in the future be such as to cause the land opposite the Cité de Refuge to be built upon, we cannot permit the Cité to benefit from the absolute maximum height of 20 meters, which the facade rue Chevaleret would still exceed considerably. . . .

—For these reasons and in spite of the philanthropic aim of the Salvation Army, we find it impossible to authorize such great exceptions to the street codes, exceptions which are moreover not justifiable by any aesthetic criteria.

(After this comment, Le Corbusier scribbled "Merci.")

—Considering our obligation to respect the regulations set forth, we feel that this code should be applied particularly to buildings constructed on land owned by the City of Paris.[16]

This official refusal, based upon technicalities and the hypothetical proposition of future construction on vacant land opposite the site, did contain insidious allusions to the aesthetic character of the projected Cité, quite as Le Corbusier claimed. There was no choice but to modify the upper portion of the building.

Alterations Due to Regulations

Three months later (April 1931) with construction already under way, the architects again wrote to the *Préfet*, stating that the building permit granted in December 1930 permitted construction of the edifice up to the third floor, and they wished to ask once more for a tolerance concerning the upper stories. They acknowledged having altered their original project to conform to the regulations applying on the rue Chevaleret, but wished to exceed these concerning the rue Cantagrel, where the facade was to be situated at a distance of 19 meters back from the street and had projecting bay windows or cornices as allowed by the code. The new proposal sent to the *Préfet* provided for a facade with extended 40 centimeters beyond that which was allowed. The administration refused to reconsider, which engendered the following solutions for bringing the two facades into conformity with the law: a setback was created on the rue Chevaleret between the third and fourth floors (sixth and seventh levels) in the form of a terrace accessible from the upper story by a small stairway; there were setbacks again on the sixth, seventh, and eighth floors (the ninth, tenth, and eleventh levels). Secondly, the glass curtain-wall of 1,000 square meters on the rue Cantagrel facade was tilted backwards slightly in order to come within the height limitation.

This continuous steel and glass curtain-wall was apparently the only item preventing the delivery of a building permit for the remainder of the structure above the third floor. However, we shall see that this airtight facade was later to be found illegal, for other reasons. What the architects decided to do was quite ingenious. They reduced by a few centimeters the cantilever of the floors from the first floor to the sixth floor (as one moved up the facade). The plane thus established by the curtain-wall sloped a total of 0.40 meters towards the interior of the building, and its uppermost edge fell within the arc of a circle by which the height limit was determined. (The radius of this circle was always established from a center point located 10 meters back from the street alignment). Nevertheless, it was also necessary to reduce the projection of the slabs on the seventh and eighth floors, at which point the facade of the upper two stories could no longer be treated simply as the logical continuation of the glass curtain-wall of the five lower levels. Hence, a new aesthetic solution seemed imperative for finishing off the top of the Cité de Refuge.

A totally different architectural treatment was therefore proposed for the seventh and eighth floors, more sculptural in quality, which acted something like an entablature terminating the glassed-in volume below. The floor surface available for use was consequently diminished, and it is possibly for this reason that the child-care center was brought down to the fifth floor, the topmost floor behind the glass facade; the last two floors were henceforth devoted to rooms for mothers with babies (in the western portion) and apartments for personnel (on the east). The slab floor of the seventh floor was conceived and executed in a sawtooth manner along the southern edge, forming a succession of spaces on the sixth floor that were enclosed by slightly convex walls of brick covered with cement, pierced by large conventional windows. Windows giving onto flower boxes were placed in the indentations (see plan, illus. 64). On the floor above, a little further back from those of the sixth floor, the walls were on the contrary slightly concave, providing usable individual terraces and flower boxes for some of the rooms.

The eastern portion of the sixth floor was handled somewhat differently beyond the large bay windows of the stair and elevator landing. The facades were parallel to the main facade, but set back slightly and contained large bay windows. Behind these were men's toilets and a large dormitory space divided by partitions into individual stalls for men, apartments for the Director and other personnel. The eighth floor, provided with one small apartment for personnel, was intended to be employed as a roof terrace-solarium for children. (It was rarely, if ever, used by them.) As a whole, this upper section of the building is articulated in such a way as to crown or frame the glass facade, between the sequence of pure geometric volumes of the ground level social services area and what we might term a sequence of tiny "garden villas" for individuals above. The confrontation of the architects' original, idealized, and primarily aesthetic solution with the city building codes produces a transformation which, in the last analysis, embodied Le Corbusier's ideological concern for an architecture that would express the dialectic between individual human aspirations and those of the community.

87. The Cité de Refuge under construction.

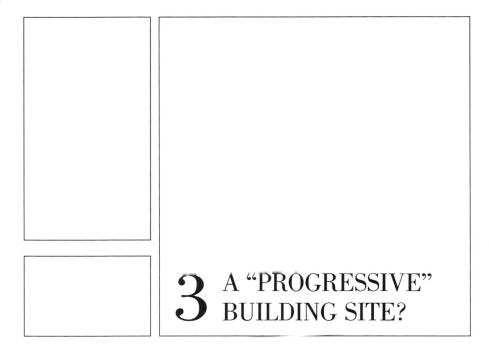

3 A "PROGRESSIVE" BUILDING SITE?

■ For without the rational capitalistic organization of labour, all this, so far as it was possible at all, would have nothing of the same significance, above all for the social structure and all the specific problems of the modern Occident connected with it. Exact calculation—the basis of everything else—is only possible on a basis of free labour.[1]

The real tragedy of Le Corbusier's activities as a practicing architect is manifest in the confrontation (which became recurrently evident even to him the more he built) between his ideology of progress, imbued with capitalist ethics, and the level of technical reality with which he had to deal. An analysis of the productive forces that actually built the Cité de Refuge reveals this disparity between the architect's innovative conceptions and his qualified success in influencing productive processes. Moreover, we find that various inherent contradictions in our history are explainable by the way in which class consciousness is manifestly apparent in the reaction of the users of the building. They, along with the workers who helped execute the Cité, consciously or perhaps instinctively at first rejected its doctrinal character, that is, the architectural and urban ideals contained in Le Corbusier's social *plan;* it was not a conspiracy on their part, but simply an inevitable phenomenon given the antidemocratic, coercive dimensions of the scientific rationalism espoused by the architect.

75

The Structure of the Cité

The structure itself, the methods of on-site construction, the mechanical services, and the social program of the institution are intimately related within the architect's total conception of the Cité. The skeleton of the principal building consists of a series of reinforced concrete slabs, approximately 80 meters long, supported by concrete columns. This framework was enclosed along the northern facade with hollow bricks and a cement coating, and with a steel and glass curtain-wall through five successive floors on the southern facade. The other smaller buildings, including the rotunda and social services block, had the same structural characteristics but employed a variety of glazing, especially large quantities of translucid glass bricks for infill. Interior separating walls—which had no structural role whatsoever—were usually of cement block and plaster, or occasionally of glass.

Supporting columns varied in diameter, according to the load they had to take, in a building that rose 38 meters above its foundations. These columns had two kinds of sections: one was composed of two half-circles with a straight portion in between them; the other was completely round. (See illus. 88). The former was employed particularly at the lower pilotis level, and although the grid of columns appears uniform on the plans, there are appreciable differences (10–15 cm.) in the thickness of certain ones. These differences are dissimulated visually thanks to the particular form which they have, being rounded on each side with a flat section in between. Special metal formwork with rubber joints was designed for both kinds of columns, which produced extremely smooth surfaces after dismantling of the forms, leaving practically no traces of the joints or of gravel deposits.

Floor slabs of the main building on the other hand, which totaled 7,800 square meters, were of a composite nature. (See illus. 88). They consisted of hollow ceramic bricks 15 cm. thick laid on wooden formwork with reinforcing between them, subsequently covered over with concrete. While the transversal beams are left visible, the joists for most floors are incorporated within the slab, which necessitated placing the hollow bricks parallel to the beam in rear portions of the slab, because of the reinforcing cables. Slabs are cantilevered approximately 1.25 meters beyond the columns along the southern facade, and carry relatively important loads. The console, or lip, along the edge of this cantilevered part was designed in such a way as to accommodate the metalwork of the curtain-wall to be attached to its outer face; in addition, it has a special profile in the form of a trough that was intended to catch condensation from the interior surface of the curtain-wall, as well as the water used to wash the tile floors.

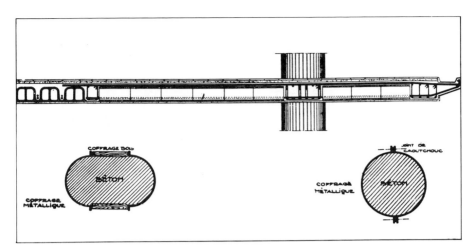

88. Section of a typical floor, showing cantilever of 1.25 meters along the southern edge whose special form was designed to receive the glass curtain-wall as well as to collect condensation on the interior. Sections of two typical columns in reinforced concrete, poured in metal formwork which could be adjusted to obtain variable thicknesses and absolutely smooth surfaces. (From *Le Batiment Illustre*, 1934)

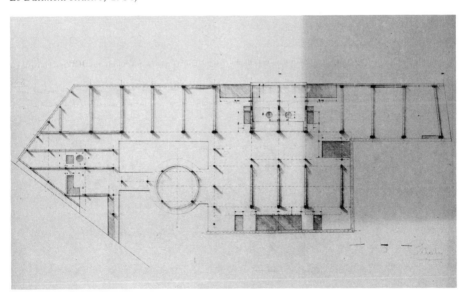

89. Plan of the reinforced concrete structure showing columns with various sections, the principal support columns and areas for elevators, stairs, and ducts (in dark hatching).

90. The metal framing for the glass curtain-wall and balconies on the southern facade, under construction.

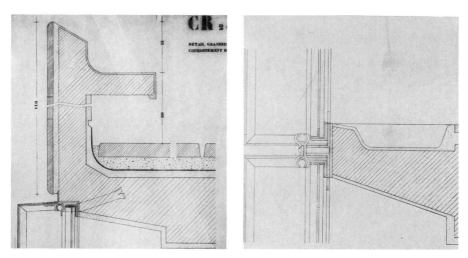

91. Section no. CR 2636, showing cornice of roof terrace and the manner of attaching the curtain-wall to the structure. FLC 10737.
92. Section no. CR 2628, depicting the system of attaching the curtain-wall to the end of each floor slab. FLC 10732.

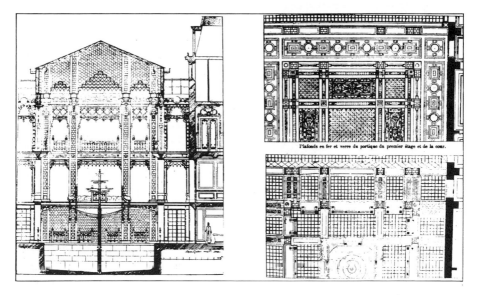

93. Section of a "Glass House" designed by Theo. Gauthier and published by Jules Henrivaux in 1894. A metallic structure has glass brick infill.

94. Ceiling plans of the "Glass House."

95. Worker constructing a panel of glass bricks called by the trade name "Nevada." (From *Glaces et Verres* magazine, 1930)

The Curtain-Wall

The *tour de force* in Le Corbusier's conception was the airtight curtain-wall of 1,000 square meters on the southern facade of the dormitory building. Carrying to its logical conclusion the principle of total independence of the means of enclosing a building from its structural system, the architects here extended the strip windows (*fenêtres en longueur*) of their 1920s villas to reach not only from column to column but also from floor to ceiling. Such a solution, harking back to ideal models that include Mies van der Rohe's skyscraper project (1920) and Gropius's Bauhaus machine shop (1926), had only been formulated and detailed working drawings made by Le Corbusier's office in 1928 for the Centrosoyus office building in Moscow. There, he proposed what he called the "neutralizing wall," a double, glass curtain-wall with air circulating in the space between the two glass walls. According to Le Corbusier, this arrangement allowed for excellent thermal insulation, since the air was to be circulated mechanically and its temperature controlled to respond to exterior climatic conditions. Moreover, in addition to providing maximum natural lighting for interiors, heat rays passing through the glass wall could be obtained in order to aid in heating the interior air. (It is interesting to note that the Soviet architect Moses Ginsburg was also experimenting at the same moment with double glazing in his Narkomfin building.) However, in the Centrosoyus as well as in the Cité de Refuge, the hermetic double "neutralizing" wall and the accompanying heating-ventilating system proved too costly for the client, and so in the Cité only a glass wall of a single thickness was ever projected and subsequently executed.

Glass Bricks

Molded glass brick was another, less conventional form of glass used in the Cité de Refuge. In the history of glass in general, and of its development in European building, the hygienic attributes of this material are emphasized already in the late nineteenth century. This important aspect is described by Jules Henrivaux—whose works we know Le Corbusier had consulted—in the following manner:

Air, light, visible cleaning, these are the things which only the use of glass allows us to achieve and which clearly indicate the role that glass can and should play as the principal hygienic agent and aid.[2]

It was only at the end of the last century that a glass modular element, measuring approximately 20 cm. on each side and 4 cm. thick, became economically feasible in vast quantities. It was initially utilized in industrial buildings (railway stations, factories, garages), exhibition pavilions or in stairwells, as in Auguste Perret's apartment building on the rue Franklin in Paris (where Le Corbusier had worked in 1908–9). The first authentic "glass house" (*maison de verre*) was projected in 1894 by Henrivaux and the architect Charles Gauthier but never built;[3] the idea was taken up again in 1929–33 and achieved for the Dalsace family, according to plans by Pierre Chareau.[4] The Dalsace house, the construction of which Le Corbusier was able to follow closely on his way along the rue St. Guillaume to and from his office, situated on the rue de Sèvres at the time, considerably influenced his own extensive use of glass bricks at the Cité de Refuge, the Clarté apartments in Geneva, and the apartment building which he was to inhabit at 24 rue Nungesser et Coli—all under design in this period.

The enclosing of vast surfaces such as these was finally made both practical and economical with the Saint Gobain company's development and marketing of glass bricks in 1928, which went under the trade name of "Nevada."[5] These had a modeled outer surface and slightly concave inner surface, which made them less heavy and more aesthetically attractive and aided in diffusing the natural (or artificial) light without decreasing the Nevada's strength.

Translucid glass bricks were employed throughout the Cité de Refuge. For instance, at sidewalk level, rue Cantagrel, they were used in order to bring light into the workshops below street level and into the entrance portico, the rotunda, and the two main dining halls at the ground floor level. They were also used to create an interior partition between the entrance hall and the offices of social workers. While they proved a successful solution for the bringing of natural light into the infirmary, which was located below grade in the garden on the rue Cantagrel, the glass bricks were a less satisfactory solution along the eastern wall and just behind the speaker's platform in the conference hall. The narrow facade of the Cité, facing the railroad yards in the rue Chevaleret, had glass bricks from floor to ceiling in the first-floor men's dining room. They had functional advantages over transparent glass in obtaining an optimal amount of diffused natural light, blocking out the view onto the unsightly industrial zone, while at the same time preventing residents from throwing things onto the street below, and needing practically no washing. Aesthetically, glass bricks provided a glittering, pristine, and uniformly modulated surface which corresponded to the image of industrialized production sought by the architects.

There were two ways of constituting walls of such bricks, both methods being employed on the building site itself: either with T-shaped metal rods running horizontally and vertically through channels along the edge of the bricks and secured with mastic to hold the individual bricks in place; or with reinforcing rods and cement, in which case the bricks were assembled by sections, in a formwork laid horizontally on a table and later taken out and mounted in place. Lack of sufficient experience with the product and a desire to reduce the joints to a minimum, for aesthetic reasons, resulted in severe cracking in the Nevadas, especially those exposed to southern sunlight, where intense heat caused them to expand.[6]

Ceramic Tiles

Finally, one should mention the fact that the architects called for widespread use of ceramic tiles in their building, both inside (for nearly all the flooring, for example) and outside (for the entry portico, rotunda, and trim on the main building). Their reasons were both functional, in the sense that tiles are durable and easily washable, and aesthetic, because they represented still another prefabricated, modular element that complemented the use of the various shapes and qualities of glass in the Cité de Refuge. This material had been reintroduced into the vocabulary of modern architecture at the turn of the century (Art Nouveau, Jugendstil) and its use, like the use of glass, had been justified by the theorists, as much for its durability and hygienic qualities as for its decorative attributes.[7] Tiles with hard smooth surfaces, easily replaced because of their shape, size, and mode of application, came to prominence in France in such buildings as that by Perret in the rue Franklin (1903), that by Henri Sauvage in the rue Vavin (1923)—both in Paris—and others.

Thermal Insulation

The exterior walls along the north facade, on the other hand, were executed in a conventional way, with hollow bricks plastered and painted over. Nevertheless, on the inside of these walls (11 cm. thick) there were panels of pressed straw insulation (5 cm.) with a 2 cm. space left for air between these and the brick wall. The composite wall (18 cm.) was said to have the same coefficient for heat transmission as a one-meter-thick stone wall.[8] It was apparently designed to keep out the chill of the prevailing northerly winds, but was also entirely without windows (except for several recessed lightwells), as the Paris building codes forbade these where the party wall was flush against the neighboring property line.

Bidding by Contractors

The gestation period in the life of this marvelous building continued, after the selection of a design, with a number of typical operations that led to its ultimate construction. The first of these was the opening of bidding to contracting firms interested in obtaining the work. We fortunately possess a handwritten table, drawn up by Pierre Jeanneret and sent to the Real Estate Commission of the Salvation Army, comparing the results of four bids submitted (September 1930) for the principal structural work.[9] A number of observations provide us with significant insights, not only into Le Corbusier's office procedures, but also into what was (and still is, in large measure) typical of the French building market.

After receiving a set of plans (floors, sections, facades) and specifications (*cahier des charges*) in which the architect establishes and explains certain requirements that must be respected, each individual contractor would proceed to analyze, to calculate, and to propose certain materials and procedures for carrying out the task at hand at a competitive price—in order to win the bidding for his company. It is at this crucial juncture that we may perceive the consequences of the traditional division of labor between the maker of plans and the engineer-builder in a capitalist market. At stake are not only the cost and the quality of the future construction, but also the economic survival of the contractor who assumes the responsibility. While the architect—in this case Le Corbusier—often advocated greater rationalization and industrialization in the building trades, he often failed to apply such concepts with the same rigor to his own method of production. Hence, the large responsibility on the architects' part for lack of precision in the documents provided to a contractor in order that he be able to estimate, for instance, as precisely as possible the costs of execution. This is where theoretical rationalization on the part of the "intellectual" architect clashed with the traditional methods and limited industrial capacity of the individual contractors.

Architects rarely calculated in detail, before the bidding, the cost of a structural system or the number of ceramic tiles of a particular type and quality needed to cover a given surface; they made only rough calculations as to costs in terms of cubic meters.[10] The Cité was estimated at 180 francs/m^3 in 1929 and ultimately cost approximately 270 francs/m^3 by 1935. Obviously, such ambiguities offered tremendous latitude for intuitive interpretation by the contracting firm, and, it might be noted in passing, this resulted in enormous differences in the prices. Most architects could not remain indifferent to this system, since their fees were based upon a percentage (normally 10 percent at the time) of the cost of construction: higher costs meant higher returns—with an additional "something under the table" from the contractor.

Four contracting firms sent bids for the concrete work of the Cité de Refuge, three (Villebière et Cie, Summer et Glauser, and Quillery) included a breakdown of their figures, and a fourth (Montocol) offered only a round sum of 7 million francs! The most revealing aspect of the comparative chart is not in the total sums proposed, which ran from 3,675,000 francs for Quillery and 4,411,000 francs for Summer et Glauser to 4,991,000 francs for Villebière, but in the large variations of price for the "same" work, broken down into ten categories (excavating, masonry, reinforced concrete, ducts, interior and exterior sheathing, etc.). For example, there was a 25 percent difference in cost for the concrete work between the Quillery first bid, which eventually won the bidding at 1,555,000 francs, and Villebière at 1,897,000 francs. Quillery's estimate for the drainage and other ducts (*canalisation*) was almost double that of Villebière (98,000 francs against 53,000 francs), and triple (37,000 francs against 12,000 francs) for demolitions and preparation of the site. The latter disparities could be attributed to the way each firm allowed margins, because of imprecise plans, while the estimates for the concrete work reflect Quillery's greater technical and organizational capabilities.

The aspect of construction, however, where the greatest variation in projected costs occurred was that of the interior and exterior finishing with ceramic tiles requested by the architects: 19,000 francs for Quillery as against 59,000 francs for Summer (with whom Le Corbusier worked habitually) for the exterior facades, and 55,000 francs versus 140,000 francs for the interior surfaces. This considerable difference in costs led the architects to ask each contractor for a breakdown of their calculations into total square meters of surface and the price per square meter. The results appear in the following schema:

	Villebière		Summer		Quillery	
Exterior facade	304 m²	94 F/m²	350 m²	170 F/m²	235 m²	83 F/m²
Interior faiences	846 m²	160 F/m²	1,000 m²	140 F/m²	470 m²	119 F/m²

Such differences, no doubt due in part to the fact that quality and cost of the ceramic finishing varies a great deal, and/or different interpretations of plans, convinced the architects of the necessity of calling in a subcontractor who was a specialist in the field.

The architects then asked each of the contractors competing for the job to determine what savings could be made if one were to (*a*) eliminate the basement garage and ramp, (b) eliminate the sixth and seventh stories, (c) do away with a projected spiral staircase, (d) replace the ceramic tiles with tiles of cement, and (e) find a more economical solution for the floor slabs. The outcome was rather inconclusive, amounting to something on the order of 10 percent savings over the original price, mostly through the elimination of the two upper stories, although the proposed use of a product called *Granitos* for the finishing of concrete floors and other interior surfaces would have resulted in a savings of 100,000 francs over the ceramic tiles asked for in the specifications; the architects refused this substitution which seemed less aesthetically satisfying to them.

The first round of bidding, which concerned only the concrete work and left for later the bidding on the curtain-wall and the rest, ended with Etablissement Quillery obtaining the contract for a projected sum of 3,954,000 francs. Stipulations of the contract[11] included the drilling of sunk well foundations four meters deep and spaced five meters apart along the northern party wall; also, an added reinforcement of columns beneath the conference hall in order to allow for the eventual addition of a wing to be constructed to the full height of the main building; the elimination of the basement garage, and finishing with cement tiles. A maximum period of ten months was specified for completion of the structure of the building, with the proviso that "It is understood that a part of the building could be available for installation to other contracting firms before the end of this period, so that the whole will be completed only slightly beyond the date we propose."[12] Thus, although the Cité was already a year behind schedule (with respect to the wishes of the Salvation Army, which had hoped to occupy the building during the winter of 1930–31), the contracting firms intended to use a rationalized system for organizing the work on the site in order to complete the operation within less than a year's time.

Rationalization of the Building Site

Much to the architect's delight, the Quillery company employed a form of Taylorism, or scientific organization of work tasks, programmed in advance, in order to achieve the superstructure of the building within a minimum period of time.[13] Various tasks were analyzed from the point of view of the optimal number of workers needed, the sequence of tasks, and the rhythm at which they could be accomplished. These analyses were expressed in the form of graphs, in which the work to be done by different crews of workmen, the one following the other, was specified, as well as the time anticipated for execution.

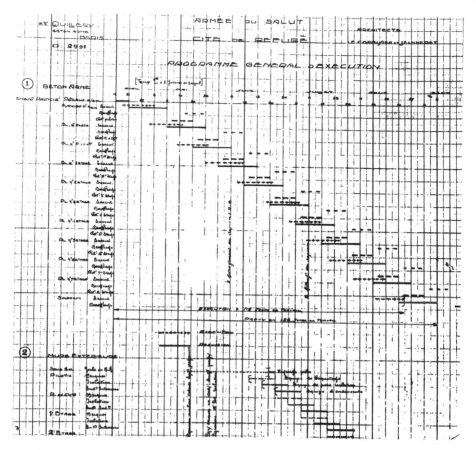

96. Graphs indicating the methods of "Taylorization" employed by the contractor for executing the reinforced concrete structure. The first diagram plots the tasks necessary for completing one floor (by thirds) against time (in days); the goal was to determine the order and rhythm of the work with an optimal number of laborers on the site at any one time. (From *l'Entreprise française*, 25 January 1932, pp. 28–29)

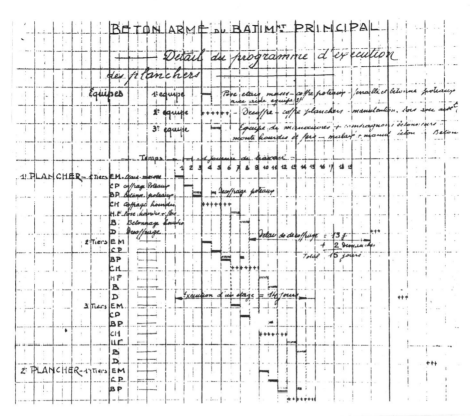

97. The second diagram shows the general program for execution, with the work necessary by floor (basement to solarium) plotted against time (in days and months); the solid horizontal lines show the anticipated time, the crosses the actual time it took (112 days).

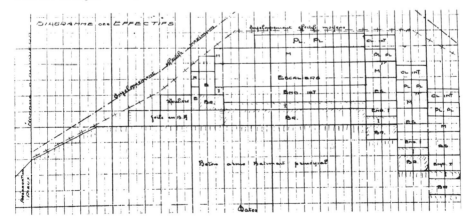

98. The third diagram shows the number of workers on the site during the entire construction period. The graphs apply only to the main building of the Cité.

99. The Cité de Refuge under construction.

100. Commissioner Albin Peyron on the building site, August 1931.

101. The roof terrace of the rotunda under construction.

102. The Cité de Refuge under construction. Upper floor with metal framing for walls between rooms for mothers with children. Pressed straw insulation known as *solomite* along the northern wall.

103. Commissioner Albin Peyron salutes the completion of the top floor.
104. The building site as seen from the rue du Chevaleret.

105. The Cité de Refuge after completion, seen from the rue Cantagrel.

Three crews were created: (1) for the erecting of the wooden form-work for columns and slabs of concrete, the placing of the steel reinforcement, and the pouring of the concrete; (2) the dismantling of the formwork, and handling of wood; and (3) the placing of hollow bricks and reinforcement for slabs and exterior walls by a crew of journeymen and concrete workers. Thus, each step in the process was broken down in such a way as to determine a method of work similar to an assembly-line, but in which the workers, rather than the product, moved from station to station.

This operation was facilitated by the fact that the building was essentially a parallelepiped nearly eighty meters long and thirty meters high, divided for structural reasons into three roughly equal sections where the expansion joints were located. In this way, one crew succeeded another, from section one to section three, until a floor the entire length of the building was terminated in a period of fourteen days.[14] Another diagram indicates the amount of personnel needed on the site at a particular moment in the construction process; the slope of the graph rises progressively during the construction of the first floor, levels off during the building of the other seven floors and then descends, as the finishing is done by plumbers, plasterers, painters, glazers, and the rest.

Foundations

Excavating took twelve days, during which 3,200 cubic meters of earth were taken out and the necessary stabilizing of adjacent buildings accomplished. On the other hand, two months' time was lost at the outset, when drilling revealed that the subsoil was unstable and a different system of prefabricated pilings were substituted for the original idea of well foundations.[15]

Tests showed that the site on which the Cité was to stand had previously been a sand quarry, extending from five meters below the actual level of the terrain, to a level two meters deeper, which was the level of the Seine River (+27 meters above sea level). However, solid rock was to be found only at +23 meters, or four meters below the level of the Seine and eleven meters below the actual level of the site. A further complication was the discovery of underground water at various levels, which caused seepage at the intended basement level of the new building. These factors made it necessary for the builder to abandon the idea of foundations made by the drilling of wells (to be filled with concrete), since pumping would be extremely expensive and he could not determine whether his foundation was sitting on the edge of the old sand quarry. If that was the case, the stability of the future edifice would be in jeopardy. Hence the decision to utilize a system of pilings, 123 in all, driven into the ground at depths of four to nine meters, with concrete footings for the columns placed on them.

These preliminary operations ran from mid-January until mid-March 1931, at which time construction of the superstructure got under way. Once the excavating and the foundations were completed, the superstructure of the Cité was constructed in 112 days instead of the 125 days forecast initially in the programming. The solarium (Level 11) was complete in mid-August, and Commissioner Peyron was able to visit the top floor of the new Cité de Refuge, with the hope that the finishing work would proceed just as rapidly. Ironically, although the consequences were not to be felt until later, the final approval of a building permit for the Cité had not *yet* been given when Peyron happily climbed atop the roof in August 1931. According to the documents, this permission was only received a month later, in September,[16] and based upon the plans provided nearly a year earlier, the only modifications having been introduced being those relative to the building's conformity with the height restrictions which had originally held up approval. Indicative though this fact is of the disorganization, not to mention the irregularity in a legal sense, of the whole operation, the critical aspect worth noting is the fragmentary, sequential manner in which the rest of the production was carried out.

Although in theory most of the remaining construction work consisted simply of assembling various prefabricated elements brought from the factory to the site, the bidding for these contracts succeeded one after the other as design proceeded, resulting in delays due to selection, availability, and utilization of certain materials and the architect's laxness in supervising the project. What in many ways was intended to be the experimental verification of certain rationalist hypotheses with regard to industrialization was compromised first of all by the irresponsibility of Le Corbusier and, second, through the irrationality of the free competitive market system as it existed then in France. This is exemplified well by the way in which contractors were chosen for the metalwork of the main curtain-wall, the rest of the metalwork, and subsequently the heating and air-conditioning installations.

In the interim the architects had decided, in the interests of a "progressive" architecture, to abandon their original designs (which had been submitted to and approved by the city) that provided for movable windows with sills, and the possibility for washing them from the inside; in place of these, they specified that only the upper part of three windows on each of five floors be able to be opened. This was in addi-

tion, of course, to the compulsory door and cantilevered metal bal-
cony situated at the western extremity of each floor. The problem initially posed for the cleaning of the exterior surfaces of windows in the
Cité was subsequently solved by means of a stage suspended from a
wagon running on rails the length of the building on the sixth floor; its
original use had been for aid in mounting the metal framework.

Four firms were invited to submit bids for the metal framing of the
curtain-wall 16.5 meters high and 57 meters long on the south facade.
Prices ranged from 189,000 francs to 317,000 francs. The two highest bids were eliminated by the architects responsible for conducting
the negotiations, probably as much because of the complexity (in
terms of individual prices) of the solutions, as their cost. The two remaining firms, Menuiserie Métallique Moderne of Reims (200,000
francs) and Dubois et Lepeu (189,970 francs) were asked to restudy
their prices, and when M.M.M. of Reims proposed a second bid of
188,000 francs, they obtained the contract.

According to the terms of the contract signed on 3 November 1931,
the M.M.M. company had until 15 December 1931 to execute the
work. Their solution entailed fixing metal channels running the length
of each floor to the concrete, and thirty, equally spaced, vertical channels measuring 40 millimeters in width. There were then two narrower
horizontal channels within each segment of the grid. Glass was to be
held in place from the inside by panels screwed into the outer framing. The system was supposed to accommodate possible expansion:

It will allow for expansion and contraction in both directions thanks to free
joints placed perpendicular to the floor slabs and a combination of iron rods
at every second vertical division; there are also two vertical joints running
through the entire height of the window.[17]

The glass facade was supposed to be entirely sealed against mois-
ture, particularly since the architects specified that a small pipe with
perforations be installed at the upper limit of the facade and running
its entire length, so that water might run over the 1,000 square meters
of glass, as a means for cooling the interior of the building.

A second round of bidding took place at the beginning of 1932 for
the rest of the metalwork, which included individual metal windows
and door frames for various parts of the building, hand rails, and so
forth, and in this instance it was the Dubois et Lepeu company, eliminated at the end of the previous competitive bidding, which was
awarded a contract for part of the work. Still another firm, that of the
Wanner family in Switzerland, for whom the Clarté in Geneva was
being built, was given part of the metalwork to execute. While the
first two contractors were paid nearly 10 percent of the *total cost* of the

building, by 1935 (456,645 francs for M.M.M. and 290,000 for Dubois), this dividing up of the labor among several enterprises is representative of how production was accomplished. Bids for the installation of glass went the same way: four firms tendered bids in January, with differences of as much as 8–10 percent in their estimates. The highest bid was from the company Célio, which had already done work for Le Corbusier and the Salvation Army, and although the next-to-lowest bidder, Beaudement, secured the contract in question, Célio was brought in later for painting and some glass work. While one might be tempted to observe that this system spread the work among many firms and encouraged competitive estimates, it certainly did not improve methods of accurate control and calculation or the efficient utilization of standardized building components.

Heating and Ventilation Systems

If the glass facade of the Cité was Le Corbusier's aesthetic *tour de force*, its correct functioning (and what one might call the veritable "motor" of this "factory for well-being") was intimately linked to the mechanical system for heating and air-conditioning the building. While central heating for apartment buildings was in relatively limited use in France, air conditioning was even more rare in 1930, and it is even today, in contrast to the United States. Air conditioning is utilized mostly in large public buildings but on an extremely limited basis in residential buildings. The architectural press of the time, as well as the building codes, attest to the fact that such mechanical systems were still at a developmental stage.[18]

A significant historical fact concerning the Cité de Refuge is that the architects had apparently decided as early as June 1930, when the project was presented, to include a system of closed circuit air conditioning, but it was only in April 1933, when the building was nearing completion that a specific kind of installation and a contractor were selected. Three years went by without a decision, even though the architects had sent out plans to various firms as early as January 1931 to obtain estimates of costs. Perhaps it was because of the extremely high initial estimates that the architects finally procrastinated; nonetheless, it should be noted that the building itself was not designed a priori to accommodate in the most efficient way possible the air-conditioning system. Installation of machinery, conduits, thermostats, and so on, came "after the fact"!

Yet so strong was Le Corbusier's theoretical conviction of what he termed "exact breathing" as the basis of physical well-being, that he invoked it as a key element for progressive modern architecture and urban planning. He consulted at least six different companies, some of which gave him comparative estimates of conventional heating installation versus air conditioning. For example, in January 1931 the Etablissements Leroy studied four different installations, the most expensive of which was 1.2 million francs for a system of forced heated air and the cheapest 500,000 francs for conventional radiators with hot water (but no special ventilation system).[19] Several months later, the Sulzer company estimated it would cost 1,640,000 francs for a combined forced air and ventilation installation, and 870,000 francs more to add a cooling system for the summer—thus, 2.5 million francs for a building just beginning construction and then budgeted to cost between 4 and 5 million! The particularly high nature of these estimates was undoubtedly due in part to the limited degree of technical development in the field but certainly also due to the variety of room sizes and types of fenestration in the Cité de Refuge, as well as the distribution of these spaces, and finally to the architects' unfamiliarity with the technology they wished to employ.

Only in May 1933, six months before the announced date for inaugurating the Cité, did the architects settle upon the proposal of the Compagnie de Chauffage Central par le Vide, which set a price of 470,000 francs for a mixed system of steam heating, mainly with blowers for areas with artificial ventilation, and with radiators for rooms with natural ventilation. The system, still common today, which was finally installed had the following characteristics: three oil-burning boilers in the basement of the building heated the air to temperatures between 60 and 105 degrees centigrade, which was carried in conduits to blowers located at critical points throughout the building; these blowers were situated next to conduits that brought fresh air from the top of the building, where it had been filtered. The electrically driven blowers mixed the moisture-laden hot air and fresh air in the amounts and the temperature desired and forced it either directly into large spaces (dormitories, dining rooms, and such) or along conduits in the corridors to individual rooms, where there was an outlet placed in the wall above the door. There were eight independent circuits, so that they could be shut off separately when dormitory or dining spaces, for instance, were not in use. Rooms did not have individual extractor-fans; used air went out under the door (or down the wash-basin pipes) and was collected by exhaust fans at strategic points. In the wintertime, they were guaranteed to evacuate cold at the rate of 1 × the volume of the room per hour; in summer, the change of air occurred at 2 to 3½ × the volume of the space per hour. There was no *accompanying refrigeration system for cooling air in the summer*, the sole provision being the possibility of opening completely the fresh air conduits from the roof and using the blowers to circulate the air. This arrangement, and the lack of an efficient system for extracting air, were the weak points in the solution adopted.

Modifications of the Crèche

The construction of the Cité de Refuge, interrupted for nearly a year, according to the testimony of Pierre Jeanneret, progressed rapidly after the decisions on heating and ventilation were made, and the details of finishing off and furnishing the interior of the building could be executed. While the interior arrangements of variously shaped lower buildings (entrance pavilion, kiosk, rotunda, meeting rooms) had already been more or less decided prior to construction (see Project 5), the modifications required in the height of the dormitory building had called into question the designation of certain spaces for specific uses. This is the case of the child-care center (crèche) for children of the single mothers residing in the Cité de Refuge and working during the day, and originally projected for the seventh floor just beneath the roof terrace. Preliminary studies for the crèche, and even the plans sent to the city administration for the building permit, indicated a long, narrow area for the purpose of such an installation but left it undefined. This was the *first* facility of this type to be designed and executed by Le Corbusier, but it appears to have been left until the last stages in the process of finishing off the Cité.

The crèche of the Cité de Refuge is a significant element within the total context for numerous reasons: in the first place, there were—and still are—relatively few such facilities in Paris, and at the time it was perhaps the only one of its type in this outlying working-class neighborhood of the city; second, Le Corbusier, in his own architectural and urban planning doctrine for the "Radiant City" of the future, considered it a principal social and recreational facility; and third, we are able to trace his concrete resolution of the problem through the documents and the building history.

In addition to being able to verify that the crèche was destined for the seventh floor at the time that the concrete construction was being completed in 1931—the exterior staircase that was to link it to the roof terrace was actually erected on the main facade and then subsequently demolished—we have study sketches for the organization of the crèche which date from the period when Le Corbusier was supervising (rather inhabitually) the building site, ordering furniture, deciding the paint scheme, and so forth, for the rest of the Cité. On the same size (15 cm. × 18 cm.) pieces of notebook paper as his notes of visits to the Cité to oversee the contracting work, one discovers a series of sketches of existing child-care centers in Paris, public and private, which the architect visited in order to become familiar with current practices and equipment. These thumbnail studies of real-life situations—often very amusing, with a nurse, for example, feeding a child or surveying children sitting on their toilet bowls—nevertheless include plans for the arrangement of rooms and verbal descriptions of essential activities (washing, eating, sleeping, wiping noses, bowel movements, playing). He asked his friend and associate in various endeavors, Doctor Pierre Winter, to recommend the model crèche facilities to be visited, such as the Salpêtrière Hospital and the Magasins du Louvre.[20]

However, as interested as Le Corbusier seems to have been in the numbers, kinds, and relationships of different rooms in a crèche, he does not seem to have consulted the literature that was available on this institution that was already a hundred years old in France, nor to have altered his original conception of locating his crèche on the seventh floor.[21] Doctors Variot and Préhu, for example, indicated in 1909 that it was much preferable to choose the ground floor for installation since circulation was much easier there, and both mothers and the crèche personnel were less easily tired out. Moreover, such a location was much better isolated from the rest of the building, since continuous circulation in a stairwell facilitated contagion. In addition, where outside play areas were possible, the ground floor installation provided more direct visual access than a location on an upper floor. Le Corbusier seems to have been ignorant of the practical advice of the specialists and, as we shall see later, it came back to haunt him.

His studies of 1932 or early 1933 for the layout of a crèche in the western half of the seventh floor of the Cité consisted essentially of an office for the director on the landing in front of the elevator (next to the chute for dirty linen); an entrance hall with individual lockers where the children changed their street clothes; and then a series of rooms, one after the other: workroom, kitchen, playroom/refectory, and two dormitories, separated from the southern, glass facade by a passageway. There were four balconies indicated, placed on the roof of the roomettes of the floor below. This proposal, of a crèche for only twenty-two children, was probably abandoned when the limitations of space became evident; it was then decided to place the crèche two floors below, on the fifth floor, where the maximum depth of the main building offered greater usable surface. In this solution, a center to accommodate sixty children was created, situated just behind the

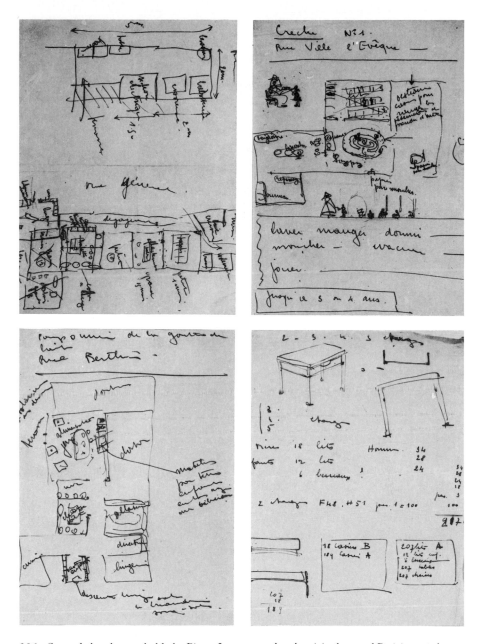

106. Several sketches probably by Pierre Jeanneret when he visited several Parisian crèches as preparation to design of the Cité de Refuge crèche. FLC 11605.

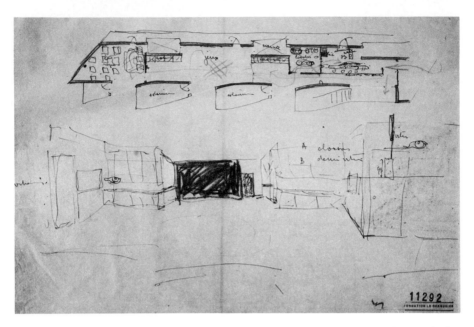

107. Plan and perspective sketches by Le Corbusier of the installation of a child-care facility on the seventh floor of the Cité, circa 1932. FLC 11292.

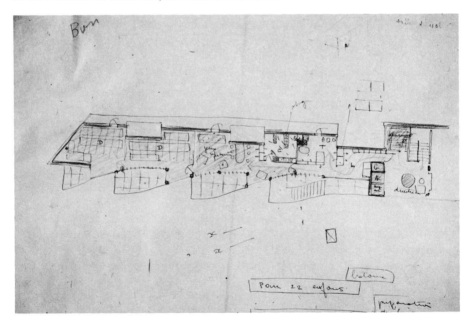

108. Plan sketch by Le Corbusier for the crèche on the seventh floor, with exterior stairs linking it to the solarium on the south facade.

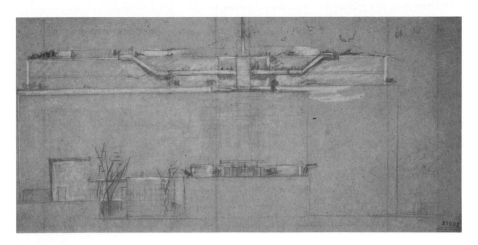

109. Study elevation in pencil and chalk of the entrance and rotunda and three upper stories. Note the treatment of forms resembling naval architecture.

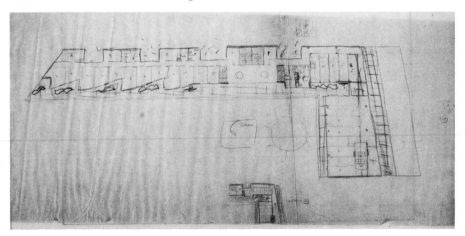

110. Plan sketch of sixth floor roomettes for mothers with a child. Note proposed extension of the Cité to the south along the rue du Chevaleret, a passing hypothesis which was not retained.

111. Axonometric sketch of the three upper stories of the Cité: the sixth and seventh are devoted to roomettes and the eighth to a solarium. FLC 11387.

great curtain-wall, yet further removed from the roof terrace play area. The director's office was isolated from the landing, and two passageways were provided, one along the glass facade and the other *between* the work areas on the north facade and the partitioned sleeping and play areas. Clearly, the nature of the building's structure allowed the architect to devise a "free plan" once the building was nearly finished; yet once again, the hurried production of plans barely preceded their execution by craftsmen dependent upon the designer's will.

Surcharges and Architects' Responsibilities

This practice of merely resolving problems as they appeared was just as true for all that was movable, notably the furniture, as it was for the fixed elements. Le Corbusier's notes, which strongly suggest his personal record of visits to the site, include the names of various contractors and work to be executed, sketches of potential solutions, of colors, and furniture to be designed and ordered. Some elements of interior furnishings were ordered from what was then available on the market, but many were specially designed by Le Corbusier and his staff (particularly Charlotte Perriand and Pierre Jeanneret): bent wood chairs by Thonet were purchased, but metal tables and beds (some with special closets for the chamber-pots of mothers with children) were manufactured specifically for the Cité de Refuge, as were cabinets, work tables, and benches. This detailed description is intended simply to underline the inherent contradictions between Le Corbusier's abstract, all-encompassing theories and evocative imagery, and his methods of practice.

The architects' own inefficient manner of proceeding (perhaps because of too much work) and their consideration of each project as an opportunity for them, as members of an avant-garde, to challenge the traditional modes of operation of the building industry, often meant that the client ended up paying *more* than he ever intended for what is called today the "product development phase" and for the industry's inability to deliver what was asked of them, in terms of cost, delay, and quality.

The Quillery construction company, the one exception to this, was able to rationalize and to execute (in even less time than anticipated, it will be recalled) a production process, thanks to an ability to calculate, coordinate, and control a sequence of tasks.

Once the structure was advancing, the bidding for contracts to execute the rest of the Cité followed the traditional pattern. Typical of this was the heating and ventilating contract for which numerous bids were solicited early in the construction phase, but most were eventually deemed to be too expensive for various reasons. Only in the last stages of finishing was a contract awarded to a company with a relatively low estimate. Whether it was true in this instance or not,[22] it was not unusual for contractors to submit a low bid just to obtain a portion of the market (especially in times of economic crisis), knowing full well they were incapable of delivering the quality of performance originally demanded. The risk of poor quality workmanship was even higher when it was a matter of materials or equipment that were still in an experimental stage of development. A "sound" and prudent contractor inevitably raised his estimates as a measure of protection whenever the requirements of a job deviated at all from traditional materials and normal routines. Such were the hard competitive practices accounting for the disparity between the architect's ideal product, or prototype, and the finished product which the client received.

The initial cost estimate by Quillery (1930) was 4 million francs for a nine-month contract; the *total* cost then for the Cité was 6 million francs. The major portion of their work was done during 1931, but the building itself was not inhabitable for another two years, and a balance sheet still two years after that (in 1935) showed that they had been paid, in all, 4,800,000 francs out of the total 8 million francs the Cité had cost.[23] Thus, the heavy construction had cost only 20 percent more over the five-year period, when the total cost had risen by 40 percent over original estimates. The major causes for this are attributable as much to the architects as to the way the French building industry operated.

Le Corbusier saw the situation this way:

> The struggle is very serious against money, venal interests, and laziness on one hand, and against the avant-garde ideas of progress on the other.[24]

> Moreover, a small remark for the record: architects are not responsible vis-a-vis their clients for defects in a house, even if it is their fault. The client is supposed to be aware of all the achitect's intentions and plans, and if the client has chosen an incompetent architect, he should consider it as his own mistake. Architects' fees are so low that they cannot cover unforeseen risks, while building firms can cover them with their 25 percent margins for unforeseen contingencies.[25]

Le Corbusier felt nevertheless entitled to the serious yet haughty tone he adopted when under attack, for he had offered to give up 40 percent of what would be a normal fee from the Salvation Army right from the beginning—that is, he invested in his own ideas. This he had done with his client Henry Fruges (who then went bankrupt!) for the Pessac housing, and with other clients. He did so obviously as one way of tempting potential clients and of getting opportunities to see his theories and designs tested in real situations.[26] In the final analysis, though, the clients most likely did not economize very much through Le Corbusier's contribution to "avant-garde experimentation" and probably ended up spending more than they intended—while most of those working in Le Corbusier's office at the time went unpaid as well.[27]

112. Le Corbusier sparring with Pierre Jeanneret, circa 1930.

4 THE CONTROVERSY

■ As with the event of birth in the life cycle of humans, the dedication of a building only marks another stage of development in the process of conception, growth, decay, and death. What gives significance to the event of intended users taking possession of a building is that we add to the natural factors (climate, soil, pollution, etc.) acting upon this physical entity, the human factor: the way people maintain, modify, or even desecrate it over time. Obviously, there are many dimensions to this human factor, including the psychological image the users' minds as to its purpose, its suitability in answering their needs, and so on, and this will affect how the building is treated. Le Corbusier, as an architect, had his own attitude with regard to the users' reactions:

> The Cité de Refuge is not a fantasy; the Cité de Refuge is a proof.
> You could tell me that it's a negative proof. To which I would reply with an observation made a thousand times over: it is, that the interested persons [the Salvation Army] make a fuss and argue in perpetual confusion between their psychological reactions and their physiological reaction. They don't know at all what they're talking about; they are obsessed by fixed ideas and it is this obsession that is the cause of their protests. We, we have the obligation to ignore this and to puruse positive and scientific research with serenity. . . .[1]

Nevertheless, when an architect has been involved in designing a building that is subsequently constructed, his eventual role in its future life may be determined according to or against his wishes, de-

107

113. The inauguration ceremonies for the Cité de Refuge, with Albert Lebrun, President of France, 7 December 1933, accompanied by Le Corbusier and Commissioner Peyron.

114. The personnel of the Cité on the roof terrace of the rotunda.

115. A banquet in the women's restaurant.

116. A popular free soup being distributed to indigents in the rotunda of the Cité de Refuge.

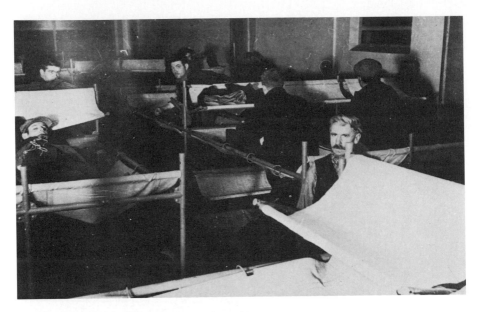

117. Residents in a men's dormitory in the 1930s.

118. A portion of the woodworking ateliers below grade level on the rue Cantagrel transformed into an assembly room for children.

pending upon the circumstances, but in France he is still responsible to the client by law for ten years after completion.

Inauguration

When the Salvation Army, client for the Cité de Refuge and the public they intended to serve, took possession on Inauguration Day, 7 December 1933, the project was already three years overdue in coming to fruition. The effort had reached considerably greater financial proportions than ever expected, and fund-raising to pay for the building was continued for some time afterwards. In this regard, Commissioner Peyron was especially gifted in procuring the necessary publicity and monetary aid from the privileged classes of French society. The building was honored that day by the visit of the President of the French Republic,[2] Albert Lebrun, and the current Minister of Public Health, Mr. Israel. Several daily newspapers carried long articles and photographs of the inauguration; one article, in *Les Temps*, merits quoting not only for the richness of the analogies evoked in connection with the building, but also for the spirit of paternalistic "good conscience" conveyed by the author:

This edifice, whose facade appears first of all like an immense glass window, has the following inscription over the entrance: "Refuge Singer-Polignac," with which its founders wish to remind us that the Princess de Polignac, profoundly moved one winter night by the distress of the outcasts to whom the Salvation Army soldiers were giving help in front of her, has given no less than 3 million francs to this enterprise. . . .

Its architects, Messrs. Le Corbusier and Jeanneret, whose fecund originality we know already, have given the edifice the appearance of a beautiful ship, where everything is clean, comfortable, useful, and gay.

The turntable at the entrance, the long counter where unhappy people will come to deposit their misery like the rich deposit their valuables at the windows in a bank. In small private offices like confessionals, they will confide in officers on duty at all hours, day and night. In this kind of "central social station" or "clearinghouse," one will direct them on their way. . . .[3]

A Question of "Exact Breathing"

The population for whom the Cité was intended, the tramps and vagabonds whose romantic existence under the bridges of the Seine had become a well-known symbol abroad, the unwed mothers, the former convicts, and the unemployed, *did* come, and they transformed the building almost immediately into an operational institution. And, almost as rapidly, there appeared the first difficulties in its proper functioning; it was not merely a question of the normal pains of adaptation but of serious imperfections in the building's conception and execution. The most critical issue which arose concerned its heating in winter and ventilation in the first summer it was in use. Le Corbusier interpreted the dissatisfaction expressed by the Salvation Army, and the public authorities they subsequently called in, as a threat to his entire theory of architecture and urban planning. He explained the situation in a letter to his patron in the affair, the Princess de Polignac:

But here we are: the Salvation Army has got it into its head, instigated by certain employees of the Cité de Refuge, to take action in the building with modifications that will purely and simply destroy the principal qualities we have obtained. I'm speaking of the intention of these Messieurs four or five months ago to open fifty or so gratings in the hermetically-sealed facade and to replace the inner circulation of vacuum-cleaned and temperature-controlled air with direct air intakes from outside, by windows. . . .

I am finishing at the moment the correction of proofs of my book *The Radiant City*, which is the sum total of fifteen years of research into the question of dwellings and the city. The fundamental chapter in the book, the keystone if you will, is precisely on the question of the lungs in dwelling places; that is to say, the quality of air to be introduced into buildings. And the fundamental hypothesis is the following: if one introduces the methods of controlled air, or lively air, or air conditioning inside of dwelling places, then a whole series of indispensible reforms could be brought about economically and efficiently. Without this, there is nothing to do; maintain the status quo.[4]

The struggle between Le Corbusier and his presumed adversaries concerning the machinery for "exact breathing" installed in the Cité became public within about a week after the building was opened:

At that moment—7 December 1933—Commissioner Peyron, wishing to exploit the technical resources of the constructed building to a maximum, made a request to the Public Health authorities, indicating that he intended to occupy all of the building in the most intense way possible, even though the regulations would be violated, and justifying this through the utilization of a system of air conditioning in the building.

On 15 December 1933, Mr. Drouet, architect at the Prefecture of Police, made a first report concerning the above request, a very intelligent report, very favorable to the building, noting that all of the rooms were in fact *anti-regulation*, but that under such conditions, it seemed to him that the logical consequence would be to change the codes.[5]

Thus began a debate that was to last eighteen months, with the Salvation Army on the one hand, seeking to placate residents of the Cité who claimed that they were suffocating at nights because they could not open a window when the ventilation was turned off,[6] or the doctor who supervised operation of the child-care center, who claimed that the children were suffering from a lack of oxygen, extremely high interior temperatures (30–33 degrees centigrade), and the deprivation of ultraviolet rays from the sun; on the other, Le Corbusier attempting to block efforts to install windows that opened in his curtain-wall. The ultimate significance of the debate for the history of modern architecture hinges upon the fact that he had erected a building that did *not* conform to the codes then in force, since he believed that they should be modified and updated. The architect's conscious strategy had been to construct a building that did not conform to the plans that he himself had previously submitted to the municipality and that were approved by them in September 1931,[7] with the intention that it would become a test case for the authorities. The system employed by Le Corbusier was lawful for ventilating such places as the Lido caberet or the Rex cinema,[8] but was not yet approved by the codes for spaces that could be ventilated directly from outside, particularly dwellings.

Had the architect been supported by the client in question, he might have had a greater chance of convincing the authorities; however, Commissioner Peyron had retired and had been replaced by another officer who was not moved by Le Corbusier's arguments of an economic order, nor by the testimony of specialists procured by the architect. Particularly sensitive to the problems raised in the section of the building for mothers with small children (fifty-one roomettes, and the nursery), Colonel Isely countered Le Corbusier's "expert advice" with criticisms of existing conditions made by the doctor in charge of the nursery and also emphasized the necessity for his institution to conform to the legal codes. Citing experts who claimed that lack of air and abnormally high room temperatures of 27 or 28 degrees centigrade had a drastic influence on child mortality, the Colonel observed that these had even been surpassed during the summer of 1934. Moreover, the doctor had had tests made of the carbon dioxide content of the air in the children's dormitory and in one of the roomettes and the results had proved to be too high.[9] When the architect obstinately refused to be impressed by these tests, the Salvation Army arranged to have others made by a specialist of the Technical Services of the Seine Prefecture, which showed that

With the present system, at the end of the day towards four o'clock, when the rooms have been *un*occupied since morning, the amount of carbonic acid varies between 45 and 64 liters/100 meters,[3] while outside there is only 40 liters; and after the space is reoccupied, the amount goes up as high as 272 liters in certain rooms.

For the summer season, the system has not been developed to bring cool air into the hermetically sealed and over-heated rooms behind the glass facade.[10]

The architect responded first of all with arguments based upon the poor functioning of the mechanical installation, suggesting that the problem was essentially one of air that was too calm, which could be resolved by speeding up the turnover of air, from one to three meters of fresh air per second. He also claimed that it would be erroneous to open windows on the vast glazed facade because the air entering would not only be polluted but, having been attracted to and heated all day long by the glass wall, would also be extremely hot.

Le Corbusier then felt constrained to ask the expert advice of specialists who he knew shared his own theory, and in particular, the physicist Gustave Lyon, who had air-conditioning equipment installed in the Salle Pleyel concert hall.[11] His report on his visit to the Cité de Refuge was understandably favorable. Secondly, he consulted one Doctor Jules Renault, professor and honorary consultant at the Hospital Saint Louis in Paris where, ten years previously, he had created a model child-care center provided with air conditioning. He, too, visited the Cité and the child-care center on the fifth floor, where he found that the renewal of air at the rate of three times an hour per cubic meter was sufficient for the spaces to be considered well ventilated. As to the assertion made by the doctor in charge, Kreyts, that the airtight glass facade prevented the ultraviolet rays from reaching the children, Doctor Renault replied that in any case ultraviolet rays from the sun in Paris was a "fantasy"; mists, dust, and pollutants in the atmosphere would block these out, and not the glass, which would permit any available rays to pass through it.[12] Le Corbusier thus concluded his inquiry, which he then sent to the Salvation Army, with the proposal that they employ the money destined for opening windows on the southern facade to install a cooling system in the nursery and roomettes, something which had been deemed too costly at the outset.

Events reached a turning point in January 1935, when the Seine Prefecture officially condemned the code infractions of the Cité de Refuge and, two months later, a second prefecture (the police) ordered openable windows installed in all parts of the building, within forty-five days.[13] Le Corbusier, exasperated and desperate, tried two tactics as a last resort: one, which was entirely typical of his previous behavior, was to call upon people of political influence to support his cause;[14] and the second was to hire a court-accredited expert. As regards the former, he appealed to Senator Justin Godart, former minister and then chairman of the Salvation Army's patronage committee, in the hope that he would intervene. His letter reveals his frame of mind at the time:

Another facet of the attack against us is the open struggle at present in France, so violent, between building traditions and those who preserve them—architects, contractors, the building trades now in decline—on the one hand, and on the other those who are trying to evolve the tools necessary for our time, amid a thousand difficulties and all sorts of imaginable obstacles.

We have already come up against the public authorities with the Cité de Refuge. I do not see, personally, the origin of this converging attack of two prefectures, but it is plausible that it has a very specific origin.[15]

As for the second, a civil engineer who was at the same time accredited as a specialist in a legal court was hired to produce a report on the ventilation of bedrooms in the Cité. His conclusion was that the rooms were well ventilated in winter: hot air entered from above the doors, was drawn toward the cold glass wall, which cooled it as it descended toward the floor, and was then evacuated underneath the door. Part of the used air escaped to the outside, and part was extracted by fans near the thermostat in the hallway to be returned to the basement for purification and reheating. However, in summer, when fresh air was simply pumped into the rooms without first being cooled, it ran up against a large stagnant body of heated air by the window, moved downwards, and immediately exited under the door. To counteract this situation, he advised drilling a row of approximately sixty openings, one centimeter wide and four centimeters high, at a level of two-thirds of the height of the glass wall. These openings, which could be entirely closed in winter, would permit a through circulation of air in the summer, thereby eliminating the necessity for full-size windows.[16] Both this proposal and an estimate of the cost of installing a cooling system were sent to the Salvation Army and to both prefectures in June 1935. They were efforts to no avail. Le Corbusier was required to ask the M.M.M. company, which had originally installed the glass curtain-wall, for a cost estimate on forty sliding windows, measuring 0.90 meters in width, to be put in the upper third of each window section.

Additional Defects

Aside from chronic difficulties with the interior and exterior plumbing, due to defective workmanship at the time of installation, a progressive decay in other physical aspects of the Cité de Refuge became apparent, much sooner than it normally should have. The exterior finishing of the Cité, with ceramic tiles manufactured by the Graiblanc company, was innovative, but not so unusual as to permit one to surmise a lack of technical expertise in the execution; the apartment buildings constructed by Henri Sauvage, the Paris Metro, and other constructions had been covered with this kind of surfacing material and did not pose grave problems a mere three or four years after completion. However, individual tiles began falling off the rotunda of the Cité de Refuge by 1936. The Salvation Army reported to the architects in June 1937 that the director of the nursery felt that the children whom he brought down from the fifth floor to the garden for air and sunshine (rather than taking them to the roof terrace!) were in serious danger of being hit by falling tiles from the rotunda.[17] They insisted that Le Corbusier, as well as the contractors, take the necessary measures to repair this defect, and they refused all legal responsibility for any eventual accident.

Since both the building contractor, Quillery, and the manufacturer/subcontractor, Graiblanc, considered themselves blameless in the affair, the architects were compelled to call in an arbitrator, a firm of legal experts called Bureau Securitas. Their engineers determined that the falling tiles were due, at least in part, to the different lengths of the reinforced concrete to which they were attached; and, since the problem was limited to the southern facade, it was concluded that the high temperatures during the summer months had affected the tiles, which had been applied with mortar directly onto the concrete and were often fitted with too narrow joints between them.[18] The Securitas report, which could have been introduced as evidence in court, reiterated, for the benefit of the parties involved, the clause of the Civil Code stating: "If an edifice of a given price perishes partly or completely, either through faulty construction or soil conditions, the architect and the contractor are responsible for a period of ten years."[19] Nevertheless, it was also their opinion that in a court of justice the problem would not be considered sufficiently extensive to invoke the abovementioned clause, and that it was the Salvation Army's responsibility to maintain this part of the building at their own cost. The architects and contractors were encouraged to offer to pay 50 percent of the repairs as a goodwill gesture, in the hope of avoiding litigation. The matter was in fact settled in this way.

Modifications after World War II

The fall of France to the German armies in June 1940 brought serious restrictions to the operations of the Salvation Army and to the full functioning of the Cité de Refuge, less than seven years after the opening of its doors. Le Corbusier left Paris shortly thereafter and in January 1941 established himself in Vichy with the intention of persuading still another "authority" to allow him to put into practice his architectural and urbanistic programs. The achievement of his decade-old project, revised over the years, for Algiers henceforth became his main goal.[20]

During the difficult times of the Occupation, even less was done than during normal times for the proper maintenance of the Cité de Refuge: the dampness stains on the interior spread, as a result of the defective plumbing and the building's settling on its foundations, causing cracks around windows and doors;[21] metalwork was not pro-

tected regularly with paint; and when panes of glass in the main facade were broken, the holes were simply boarded up—or bricked up
when bricks were obtainable. As ill luck would have it, and as a last
dishonor to the "beautiful ship," the Germans dropped a bomb in
front of the Cité de Refuge, on the very day of the Liberation of Paris
on 25 August 1944. Whatever panes of glass remained in the facade
at the time disappeared.[22]

Four years passed without a major effort to rehabilitate the building,
and it was Le Corbusier himself who wrote to the Salvation Army in
1948 offering his services, free of charge, as counsel to them in restoring the Cité. He explained, by way of excusing his negligence,
that a shortage of material during the reconstruction period, and his
obligation to struggle in order to impose the concepts of modern architecture on an uncomprehending public, had delayed him in making
his offer.[20] Moreover, he added, because of his connections with the
director, he was in a position to obtain the glass needed to repair the
facade at a special reduction in cost from the Saint Gobain glass
manufacturers. When the Salvation Army responded favorably to his
proposal, Le Corbusier contacted his cousin and former associate,
Pierre Jeanneret (with whom he was no longer in partnership), who
had just returned to Paris after spending the war years in Switzerland,
and offered him the job of supervising the restoration of both the Cité
de Refuge and the Swiss dormitory. Jeanneret gratefully accepted,
with the following words:

I thank you for having thought of me. These two children are dear to me, and
I would not like to let them drop. One of them especially, the Cité de Refuge,
has suffered, I think, and even more, had certain problems at birth.[24]

This recollection by Jeanneret of the difficult "birth and childhood"
of the Cité, and of the architects' devotion to making it a successfull
endeavor, was equally matched by the client's memories of the problems caused in the beginning by the glass wall and the heating and
ventilating systems. The Salvation Army addressed a report to Le Corbusier, in which they recommended that the facade be restored not to
its original state, but instead be remodeled to include three bands of
infill on each floor from the first to the fifth, where the lower part (1.10
meters high) would be solid, the middle part would have permanently
closed windows, and the upper part would be provided with transom
windows for ventilation. Although the report conceded that the heating of the large public spaces by means of blowers had originally been
a success, they urged that the system of radiators, already partially
installed in roomettes, be extended throughout the Cité.[25] Le Corbusier and Jeanneret acquiesced to the requests of the client this time
apparently without a fight, this assent contrasting curiously with the

119. The south facade of the Cité after the bomb damage of 1944. The curtain-wall is boarded up and concrete blocks used to make rooms.

120. The south facade after renovation and addition of the *brise-soleil* in 1952.

121. The "fresco" painted over the glass bricks of the social workers' offices during a first renovation effort, circa 1950.

122. Photo of 1976 illustrating how the original metal frames for windows had been filled with bricks during previous restorations.

123. The interior of glass windows in the women's restaurant.
124. The entrance pavilion in 1976, showing extensive cracking of glass bricks due to intense heat and faulty installation.

struggle that had been so passionate, and a question of principles, in the 1930s. However, the architects proposed at the same time the construction of a sunscreen (*brise soleil*) on the southern facade of both the Cité de Refuge and the Swiss dormitory, in an attempt to control the amount of direct sunlight penetrating to the interior. The engineer Bodiansky and the designer Xenakis in Le Corbusier's office were asked to study this solution, taking into account the fact that the facade of the Cité behind the *brise soleil* would now be 60 percent opaque anyway, making the sunscreen something of a redundancy.[26]

Aesthetic values rather than functional criteria (which may even in fact explain the creation of a sunscreen) turned out to be the main area of disagreement between Le Corbusier and the Salvation Army during the restoration work. The architect, busier than he had ever been in his life with the construction of the *Unité d'Habitation* building in Marseille and the planning of Chandigarh in India, among other projects, seems to have been amenable to various transformations of his original work in order to meet the changing needs of the Cité. But he would admit no compromise whatsoever concerning his judgment on aesthetic matters. The colors he chose for the facade, based upon the colors already existing on the entrance kiosk, were the result of long and profound reflection. An indication of an impending crisis with the Salvation Army over such matters is revealed in one of his letters to Wycliffe Booth, head of the Army in France and grandson of General Booth the founder:

The color samples established in the spring are erroneous. The Salvation Army colors, which are beautiful, ought to be reproduced in their exact tonality; that is to say: dark red, dark blue, and a yellow which is composed of yellow ochre and not of chromium. The facade will sing, with the large entrance portral, and will produce a superb impression.

Someone mentioned to me putting the color grey behind the sunscreen rue Cantagrel, which would be a disaster. I should even add, dear Sir, that my artistic rights do not permit one to do anything with this facade which would be contrary to my strictest desires. In addition, this facade is well known, it was damaged by the war, it should be reconstructed and allowed to shine again.[27]

The departure of Pierre Jeanneret to India, as Le Corbusier's representative on the Chandigarh site, and his replacement on the Cité de Refuge restoration job by another architect could only have contributed—once more—to the client's impression of Le Corbusier's personal lack of interest. His frequent absences from Paris, something which had always irritated even his most faithful clients,[28] inevitably resulted in decisions being made without his approval. Trying to remedy the errors once they were committed—as in the choice of colors on the facade, with which he was not in agreement—proved to be too formidable a task for him on the day in 1952 when he visited the Cité and found that the smooth concrete columns of the entrance hall had been covered with paper that resembled imitation marble and wood, not to mention the wall of glass bricks painted over with a mural decoration. As irony would have it, it was to Irène Peyron, Albin Peyron's daughter and then Commissioner of the Salvation Army, that Le Corbusier wrote in utter disgust to resign as consultant for the restoration. Her sage reply was that nothing, not even a building, was eternal on this earth and that the present users of the Cité ought to be forgiven their errors of bad taste.[29] While this ended his collaboration with the Salvation Army for the time being, it is nevertheless worth noting that some years later, when Le Corbusier returned to the Cité (after the imitation marble and wood had been removed), his design for the interior color scheme, was followed, as it ought to have been.

A Problematic Restoration

In 1975, some ten years after Le Corbusier's death, the Cité de Refuge was again badly in need of drastic measures to restore and preserve its physical soundness. While the two main facades, on the rues Cantagrel and Chevaleret, had had their metal window frames replaced with wooden ones during the 1950s face-lifting, the original metal ones remaining in the first-floor dining rooms, the stairwells on the north, and the rooms of the two upper stories, were severely rusted and warped out of shape. At some point in the past, the floor-to-ceiling window frames of the upper-story rooms had been partially filled in with bricks and simply cemented over; the different coefficients of contraction and expansion between the metal, the reinforced concrete, and the brick had resulted in large fissures and the infiltration of dampness. Where parts of the concrete had detached themselves or worn away, the internal reinforcing rods were often exposed—a result, in part, of their having been placed too close to the outer surface. The extensive intervention needed to correct these problems, particularly on the upper stories, required the approval of the French Cultural Ministry's Commission on Monuments, since the rue Cantagrel facade (as well as the interior of the main entrance hall) had been placed on the register of protected historic landmarks.[30] Representatives of the Fondation Le Corbusier in Paris were participants in early discussions that led to the eventual approval for work to go ahead, but neither their advice nor the assembled documentary material then available were solicited thereafter by the Salvation Army or the architects.

The replacement of the metalwork—window frames, door frames, balconies, and exterior stairs—constituted one of the largest single items in the budget, mainly because they were unavailable on the market and had to be custom-made. This underscores the fact that while Le Corbusier had advocated and in some measure achieved, as we have seen, the standardization and industrialization of building components, such products were often only continued for limited periods of time and then dropped; hence, restoration of modern buildings is nearly always a job for craftsmen! Glass bricks, which provided the infill for these window frames in many instances, posed a similar problem—although the Saint Gobain company is once again manufacturing such elements, it is with different profiles and in different molds than the original Nevadas. In both cases, measurements were made and the metal frames and glass bricks brought to the site where they were assembled. The glass bricks then were composed in sections and mounted in place, following the same procedures as fifty years ago.

After preparation of the masonry surfaces, including the sunscreen, the repainting of both facades was undertaken. The radical transformation in the 1950s of the original glass facade and the introduction of polychromy had provided the Cité with an entirely new physiognomy, in partial agreement with Le Corbusier's wishes. However, once again, his previously specified recommendation as to the precise tint to be given to the three primary colors, blue, red, and yellow, were not respected. The sunscreen, which Le Corbusier had said should be left in its natural concrete state, was painted a brilliant white; so, too, were the masonry portions of the two upper stories, which (in the author's estimation) had never had such a glaring, whitewashed intensity. Only the ceramic tiles originally had this quality of opaque brilliance. Considering the expense involved for the Salvation Army, as well as the responsibility of the various interested bodies, public and private, greater effort ought to have been spent in determining, through Le Corbusier's written descriptions, his paintings, and so forth, what the true color nuances might have been for these vast and ostensive exterior surfaces.

Finally, the interior modification to the Cité, dictated by changing needs or conceptions of the way in which it should serve its residents, have been relatively minor. While the men's dormitories on the rue Chevaleret have remained almost untouched since 1933, the large, open dormitories for women have been partitioned in order to create more privacy (spaces for eight or ten beds, or individual rooms) as was the floor where the children's nursery was located until its elimination after World War II. This is in concordance with the Salvation Army's policy of seeking to provide a maximum number of individual rooms for residents,[31] as opposed to their previous emphasis upon collective living accommodations and activities.

To recapitulate the astonishing richness of this one building as a crucible of multiple intentions and conflicting values, one might first consider Le Corbusier's attitude toward the finished product and its utility. For him, the Cité de Refuge, as built, was the proof of the hypothesis that the physiological well-being of city-dwellers could be guaranteed by means of an enlightened architectural conception and mechanically controlled interior environments (i.e., high-rise glass-enclosed edifices plus air conditioning). He considered that, as an architect, he should pursue, in collaboration with other specialists, scientific research that would lead to improvement of the biological conditions for human habitation—and that the spiritual or psychological well-being would follow, maybe even reluctantly adapting itself to the "fruits" of modern technology. He coupled his physiological arguments to others, based upon the economic utility procured through environmental controls, such as savings in fuel consumption (although he did not go so far as to elaborate the notion of solar heating[32]). The architect adamantly defended the systems, however imperfect, conceived and installed in the Cité de Refuge, against all attempts by the Salvation Army to modify the conditions of his experiment on these grounds.

Twenty years later, when Le Corbusier was over sixty years of age, his main preoccupation in seeing the Cité restored seems to have been purely aesthetic in nature. Even though his theoretical ideas had evolved in that lapse of time, it nevertheless seems clear that he had less inclination to engage in polemical battles for the sake of a progressive ideal. Of greater importance for the by-then-world-renowned architect, was the preservation of a certain image of modern architecture.

The Salvation Army's view of the product bestowed upon them, on the other hand, was much more pragmatic than it was theoretical. As an institution it had not been known to patronize either avant-garde or even famous traditionalist architects, prior to their having Le Corbusier more or less imposed upon them by the Princess de Polignac. Furthermore, their policy since that time has not evolved in the same manner, for instance, as that of private industry or public authorities, which sometimes cultivate a prestige image by addressing themselves to outstanding architects. With limited budgets for each new attempt to expand their services, the Salvation Army continued the tradition started by General Booth of converting existing buildings and making additions where necessary. What they obtained with Le Corbusier was an overly expensive, malfunctioning building, the experimental attributes of which seemed merely to cause problems for the staff and services they wished to provide. It was only natural for those responsible for the Cité de Refuge to seek other avenues for modifying the building to meet their demands, when their own architect proved intractable. Moreover, the Army was a *collective* client rather than a single individual, with divers boards and committees; the heads of these, like the director of the Cité or the French commissioner of the Army itself, were replaced over time, and with these changes the interpretation of needs and priorities also changed. Thus, it must be said that modifications in the Cité were inevitable, and if they began nearly as soon as it was built, with the decision to install windows that opened in the curtain wall, it was due to the surfacing of the basic, irreconcilable conflict in points of view between client and architect. The consumer wanted a sound, sturdy product that would meet not only the spiritual but also the psychological and physiological expectations of the inhabitants, and not a fragile mechanical system which frequently provoked physical and mental discomforts. Le Corbusier's suggestion at one point that caged white mice be installed in order to test the suitability of the environmental conditions for humans "—not an uncommon practice—nevertheless reveals his lack of sympathy for the users' reactions, particularly those of the women residents living with small babies in the tiny, narrow roomettes.

A large segment of the active users of the Cité was composed of transient male residents who came to spend a limited number of hours at night on an infrequent basis. Consisting of a vast diversity of society's most marginal elements, these men, who were out of work, suffering from alcoholism or other disturbances of a social origin, could not be expected to share in any way whatsoever in Le Corbusier's technological or aesthetic system of values. Their anarchist tendencies, if in the main only passive, were directed against the very capitalist society which continued to exploit them but yet could afford to pay for a shining new refuge. That they occasionally fought with one another in front of the rue Chevaleret entrance, as was reported to Le Corbusier,[34] breaking the plate glass in the doors so that it had to be replaced, is only a minor, yet significant indication of their total disregard for a great masterpiece and the society that produced it.

Finally, there was the "objective" viewpoint of the public authorities who saw the Cité de Refuge as a violator of building codes and therefore in need of modification. Monument or no, the Cité de Refuge experienced the considerable pressure of bureaucratic procedures aimed at "normalizing" its existence. Le Corbusier's vigorous advocacy of standardization in the world came back in this way to haunt him when, in the present case, he was compelled to accept defeat in his endeavor to have the city's existing codes modified through a *fait accompli.*

125. *Clochards* seeking entry to the Cité.

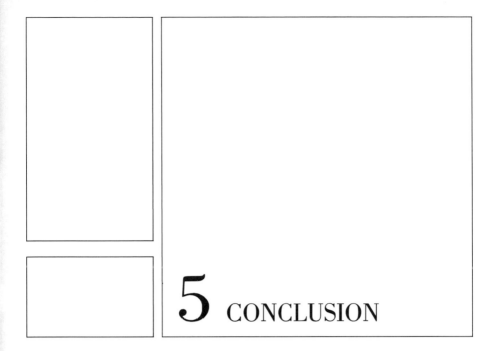

5 CONCLUSION

■ A critical analysis of the Cité de Refuge is instructive for a number of reasons. We have already mentioned three main ones which allow us to understand the significance of this "monument" within the context of twentieth-century architectural movements: first of all, its socio-economic and political significance as an architectural *type;* then, its production as a physical object (its constituent elements, process of construction, and functional efficiency); finally, the role of Le Corbusier as architect, and particularly his way of operating in concrete reality. All of these critical aspects are superimposed in the history of the building; their analysis contributes to a much-needed "demystification" concerning such important buildings and those who created them.

The Cité de Refuge as Instrument for Social Control

Neither a hotel nor a school like any other, nor a workshop nor a hospital, the Cité de Refuge once incorporated, to one degree or another, all of these socially important functions. However, as Michel Foucault aptly points out,[1] shelters like the Cité de Refuge have a close kinship with penal reform institutions, although, to be sure, they constitute a middle ground between incarceration and freedom of movement for an individual. The key attribute which such institutions have in common as *hétérotopies* (places set apart from the rest) is their quality of isolation; in the case of prisons, there is also the emphasis

127

upon *discipline* as the decisive method for reforming the soul and body of those persons considered socially marginal (i.e., sick). Discipline, according to Foucault, is exerted upon individuals by penal institutions—and, to varying degrees by affiliated organizations—according to three general models for manipulation:

The political-moral model of individual isolation and of hierarchies; the economic model of applied force for a required task; the technical-medical model of curing and of normalization.[2]

The Grand Scheme of the Salvation Army's founder William Booth, and the "Colonies" which grew out of that program, correspond in essence to Foucault's description of the way in which the mechanisms of discipline are utilized by the dominant class in our capitalist society.

The brief for the Cité de Refuge arose as part of a coordinated building campaign by the Salvation Army in France during the late 1920s. This campaign even included a proposal for building a hostel-shelter in French Guiana to accommodate recently released convicts from the Bagne de Cayenne prison, and Le Corbusier expressed interest in designing that project as well.[3] The manner in which the dominant class in France, and the State in particular, actively supported the Salvation Army's programs is evident from the list of members on its patronage committee. Economic and political motivations permeated the Army's existence from start to finish, as George Bernard Shaw so clearly perceived early in the century. That religion was an essential part of the ideology of the Salvation Army derived from the ethical value that Protestantism attached to a person's economically useful role in the society.[4] Labor signified submission to a discipline, and the production of wealth was the means by which one could hope to obtain God's approbation. The Salvation Army, with its roots in the Methodist sect, thus used two interrelated tools to rehabilitate the alienated individual: that of religious conversion, and that of labor as a daily discipline. While it did not renounce the former in favor of the latter, as did a certain early nineteenth-century prison reformer quoted by Foucault, their economic motives were ultimately similar:

If in the end [says Michel Foucault] prison work has an economic effect, it is in producing mechanized individuals according to the general norms of an industrial society: "Work is providential for modern peoples [observes the reformer in question] it takes the place of morality, fills a vacuum in beliefs, and is accepted as a principle leading to everything good. Work should be the religion of prisons. In a machine-society purely mechanical means of reform are required."[5]

While there are hierarchies of authority in the Salvation Army's organizational structure, their methods do *not* include the political-moral model employed in prisons; nevertheless, what has been described as the technical-medical model for healing and normalization *is* an integral part of their operation. Since there was, as a rule, a limit to the number of paid nights one could stay in the Refuge unless one was part of a "work-aid" program (*assistance par le travail*), those who did stay for protracted periods were morally obliged to submit to the rules and requirements of the system.

Any critical evaluation of the building itself has thus to be grounded ultimately in the very nature of the institution it was intended to serve. Spaces in the Cité de Refuge were designed to accommodate the procedures by which an individual entering the premises was progressively taken in charge by the institution's social services: from initial reception at the rue Cantagrel entry to the counseling rooms at the opposite end of the main level thoroughfare. An individual's physical health and his dress were controlled at the infirmary and clothing exchange in the lower levels of the rotunda, while his spiritual state was treated just opposite these, in the large meeting hall. Activities occurred not only in specific places but also at specific times, and some (such as eating) were regulated by bells which rang throughout the building.[6]

The Salvation Army's imposition of a pervasive collective discipline upon an individual's use of spaces and his social behavior was extended a degree further, to his body's functioning, thanks to the architect's introduction of an artificially controlled environment: the quality of the air he breathed and the temperatures of the rooms he inhabited were normalized as well. In this way architectural and mechanical engineering formed the complement to the social engineering of redemption aspired to by the Salvation Army.

Ideology and Reality of Rationalized Production

The Cité de Refuge nevertheless embodied a concerted effort of historical significance for the time to modernize not only mechanical equipment and services but also the process of building itself. For the concrete work, Le Corbusier submitted his plans to a contractor who applied methods of scientific rationalization to his labor force and finished the structural frame in less time than was foreseen. However, at the time this was only possible in certain fields of the industry, where the scale of the operation was sufficiently great to merit overall planning and where sufficient control could be carefully exercised. For the rest of the building trades, the methods of craftsmen still prevailed and concepts of Taylorism or Fordism—so admired by economic theorists and politicans of the period—were hardly known or applied at all.

The general mystification surrounding Le Corbusier and his *oeuvre* arises from the following paradox: a prolific writer, experienced lecturer, and irrepressible strategist, he extolled the virtues of efficiency and rationality in planning, while continuing to practice his profession as designer in the idiosyncratic ways of a traditional craftsman. The necessity for a *comprehensive plan* (a "Grand Scheme" in General Booth's terminology) in order to resolve the pressing problems of economical construction and structured urban development was something Le Corbusier preached but did not believe in sufficiently to apply to his office's production. In the final analysis, his ideological justifications for what he built rarely had much to do with the aesthetic power of a work or the way he went about accomplishing it.

As an architect operating on the level of daily realities, Le Corbusier had little immediate impact upon customary practices in the building industry. Like many other projects, plans for the Cité de Refuge left the office at the last possible moment, and those destined for contractors usually carried the notation, "Dimensions to be verified on the site by the contractor." While this was the usual disclamatory clause of the period, the architects played only a minor role in the actual development of new constructional techniques. The techniques for installing the 1,000 square meters of plate glass on the facade, for instance, or the glass bricks were left entirely to the initiative of the industry. A man of large ideas, Le Corbusier was prone to leave the details, particularly of execution, to his collaborator cousin, Pierre Jeanneret, and it is to him we owe the very existence of many buildings of this period. Le Corbusier lacked the capacity, or perhaps the interest, to develop the crucial knowledge that a closer relationship with the builders would have brought him—as it did Alvar Aalto, for example—thereby permitting the architect to gear progress at a conceptual level to that which the productive forces were capable of assimilating.[7]

Le Corbusier's convictions concerning scientific rationalization of production remained on an intellectual and political level. Laborers needed self-discipline, or discipline imposed upon them from above, in order to adapt themselves to the ultimately desirable results of engineering. The architect aligned his thinking to that of Ernest Mercier and the association known as "Redressement Français," occasionally giving lectures for them,[8] precisely at the moment he was designing the Cité de Refuge. His active affiliation with this group at the time he was also flirting with the Soviets bears out the latter's fundamental criticism of his position: Le Corbusier was *not* in favor of a revolution in social relationships as an indispensable prerequisite to advances in material culture. Instead, like the Redressement Français, he advocated the formation of a managerial elite of economic experts in a capitalistic society, apparently above party politics, who would plan and direct a peaceful social revolution. Impressed by the administrative techniques of Taylorism found effective in ordering industrial production and labor relations, the participants in Redressement Français felt that class conflicts could be avoided and economic progress attained through social engineering; it was only a matter of making the workers understand and accept certain necessities.

Le Corbusier found common ground for cooperating with and serving the needs of the Salvation Army, precisely because he shared their attitudes towards the economic necessity for social engineering. Reform of society as of individuals, whether psychologically or in terms of their economic utility, would be best accomplished according to technical-medical methods of control. Where the client and architect found they differed was over the persuasiveness of *mechanical* means, namely an airtight building with malfunctioning machines for heating and ventilating. Le Corbusier's reaction to the protests of the women who objected to being unable to open their windows in the Cité (his attitude of "We have a moral right to ignore them and to continue scientific research!") put him at odds with the Salvation Army; but it also raised the fundamental issue of technocracy, of the political principles that would eventually govern the relationship between men and machines.

Le Corbusier's position was criticized from a Marxist point of view in 1933 by S. Gournyi, a Soviet architect. His statement, grotesque at times, contains a number of insights into pervasive ambiguities in Le Corbusier's thinking. It warrants quoting *in extenso:*

We have already cited the cause: it is the dual conception of Le Corbusier. When the individualist tendency of capitalist society runs strongest, he is attracted by the idea of small cottages on pilotis, at 1,000 persons per hectare, but with a total, sealed isolation of mankind.

Man is perpetually striving to free himself from collectively imposed constraints, tending to remain alone with himself. Each house in this case could easily be seen as an *asylum*, which has to be independent, closed, private, and *sacred*. The family ought to be able to live exactly as it pleases, to live its individual life without any *collective* restraint.

When Le Corbusier imagines society as a whole, he is inclined to admit society's rights over its individual members. He voices the opinion himself that sports should be imposed in the interests of physical improvement of society's members. But when he drops this notion and begins to reflect on the interests and feelings of separate individuals, taken in isolation, then collectivized society appears to our architect as a barracks with coercive rules and regimented mentality. At that point, he rebels.

However, the essential point is certainly the difference between the two systems' conception of the world, the expression of different social systems. We subordinate all transformation of material culture to that of social organization. Le Corbusier sometimes gives the impression that he shares this point of view, albeit partially, when he discusses advantages of collective forms of community life and when he continues to develop and to analyze our way of seeing things. Yet, as we have already noted several times above, he suddenly falls back under the influence of social and ideological conceptions of an individualist, bourgeois society and tries to resolve issues separately, outside of an overall system—or rather on the basis of the existing system; a certain perfecting of what already exists is the result.

It is obvious that the panaceas proposed by Le Corbusier mentioned above are only a reaction against the state in which our large cities find themselves today. Only such a Leviathan, grinding away with continuous movement night and day, could give birth to the idea of an *asylum* made of steel, hard and tightly sealed. Only the overcrowding which characterizes this octopus and the poisonous air it exhales could have provoked the notion of "artificial respiration." Only the abnormally excited nervous system of an inhabitant of a large capitalist city could stimulate the terrible need to lock oneself up, to isolate oneself in an airtight, *sacred asylum.*[9]

This argument, which at moments borders on caricature, nevertheless raises the essential problems in a forceful manner: whether or not we are to subordinate material culture to social relationships; whether or not the Cité de Refuge, inspired in part at least by collectivist dwelling units in Russia of the period, and the subsequent "Unité d'Habitation" proposed by Le Corbusier are to be interpreted as viable expressions of a world of altered, progressive social relationships. Is a project such as the Cité de Refuge for lodging a complete, highly structured, and "self-sufficient" social unit part of a larger dialectical method on the architect's part? Or, in the final analysis, does it simply correspond to the work of the Salvation Army itself, to wit, the creation of necessary "sacred" refuges where the socially ill can be re-formed and reintegrated into a capitalist economic system?

126. View of the rue Chevaleret facade (left) after restoration in the 1970s, with adjacent annex (right) by another architect.

APPENDIX
THE CITÉ DE REFUGE
AS COMPLETED AND
AT PRESENT

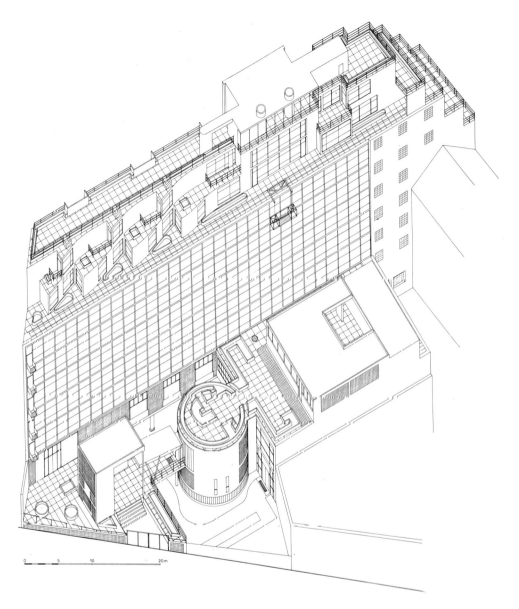

127. Axonometric view of the Cité de Refuge as constructed. (Drawn by H. Lapprand)

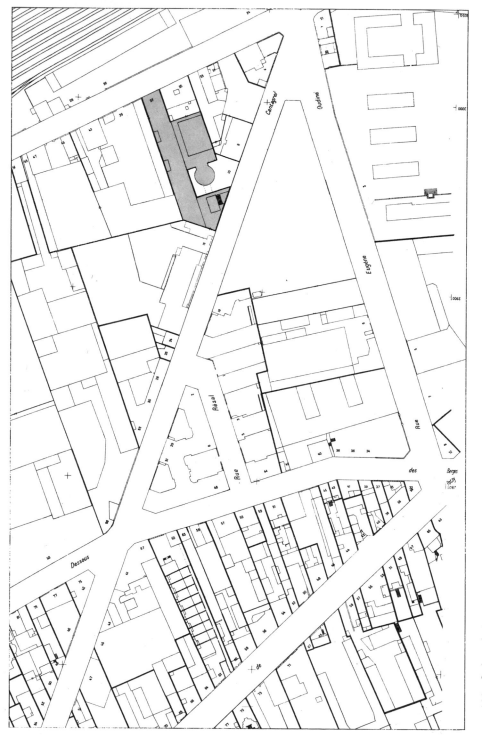

128. Cadastral plan of the neighborhood where the Cité is located. Scale 1/1,000.

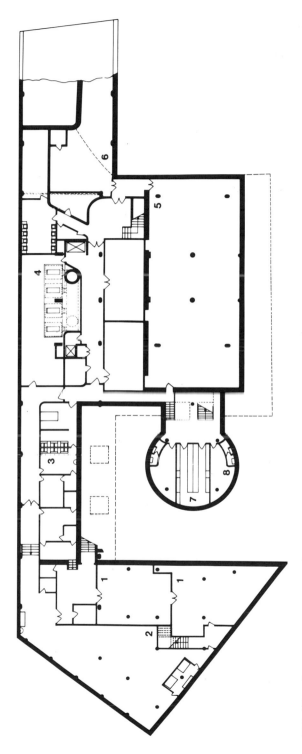

129. Plan of basement as constructed: *1.* women's workshops; *2.* men's workshops; *3.* laundry; *4.* heating machinery; *5.* salesroom; *6.* ramp to garage; *7.* clothing exchange; *8.* disinfecting room.

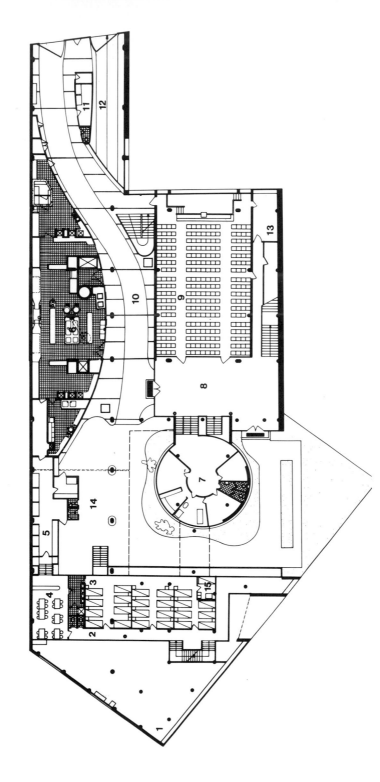

130. Plan of pilotis level: *1.* empty space over workshops; *2.* mezzanine corridor; *3.* elderly women's dormitory; *4.* refectory; *5.* storage; *6.* kitchen; *7.* dispensary; *8.* hall; *9.* conference hall; *10.* driveway; *11.* guard, control booth; *12.* garage ramp; *13.* office; *14.* covered area; *15.* superintendent.

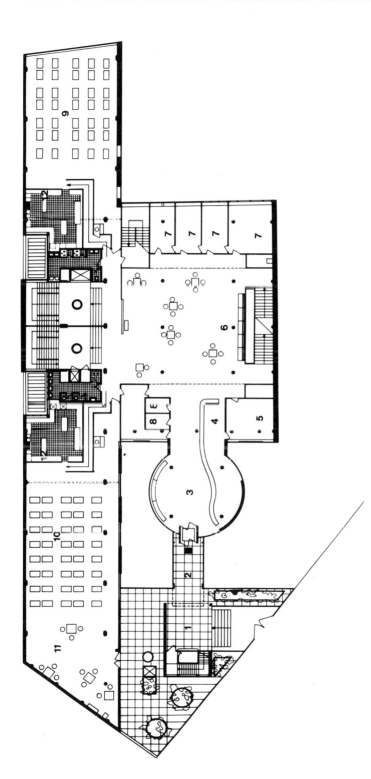

131. Ground floor plan: 1. entrance portico, guard; 2. bridge; 3. orientation desk; 4. cashier; 5. director's office; 6. great hall; 7. social services; 8. offices; 9. large men's restaurant; 10. women's restaurant; 11. women's lounge; 12. serving area.

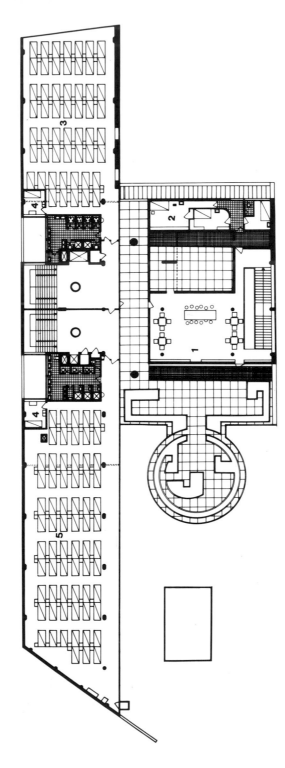

132. First floor plan: *1.* library/men's lounge; *2.* apartment for personnel; *3.* men's dormitory; *4.* superintendent; *5.* women's dormitory.

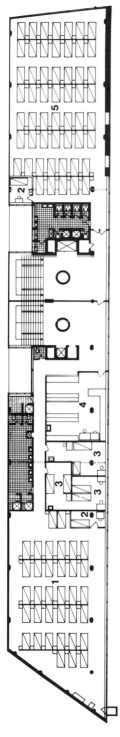

133. Second floor plan: *1.* women's dormitory; *2.* superintendent; *3* roomettes with two beds; *4.* laundry; *5.* men's dormitory.

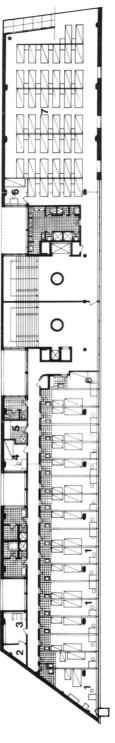

134. Third and fourth floor plans: *1.* roomettes for mothers with a child; *2.* drying rooms; *3.* laundry; *4.* private room; *5.* room for preparation of babies' bottles; *6.* superintendent; *7.* men's dormitories.

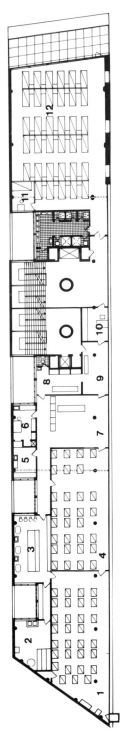

135. Fifth floor plan: *1.* infant's dormitory; *2.* laundry, crèche; *3.* children's toilets; *4.* older children's dormitory; *5.* doctor; *6.* food preparation; *7.* playroom-refectory; *8.* reception; *9.* hall; *10.* director's office; *11.* superintendent; *12.* men's dormitory.

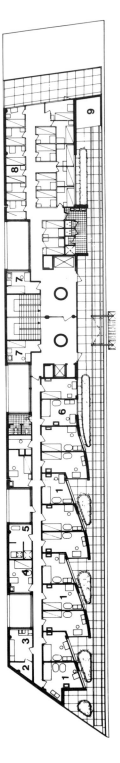

136. Sixth floor plan: *1.* roomettes for mothers with a child; *2.* drying room; *3.* laundry room; *4.* milk preparation area; *5.* nursing room; *6.* Princess de Polignac's room; *7.* superintendent; *8.* roomettes for men; *9.* garage/window-washing rig.

137. Seventh floor plan: *1.* director's apartment; *2.* laundry; *3.* milk preparation area; *4.* rooms for mothers with children; *5.* personnel; *6.* nursing; *7.* principal director.

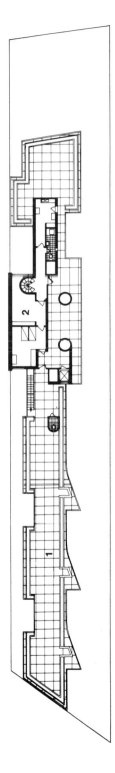

138. Eighth floor plan: *1.* solarium; *2.* assistant director's apartment.

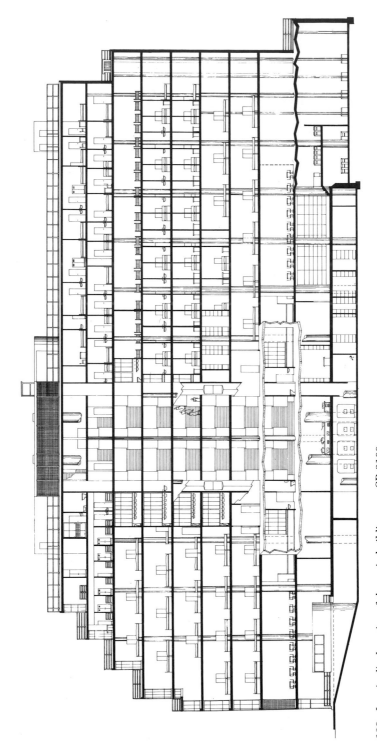

139. Longitudinal section of the main building, no. CR 3100.

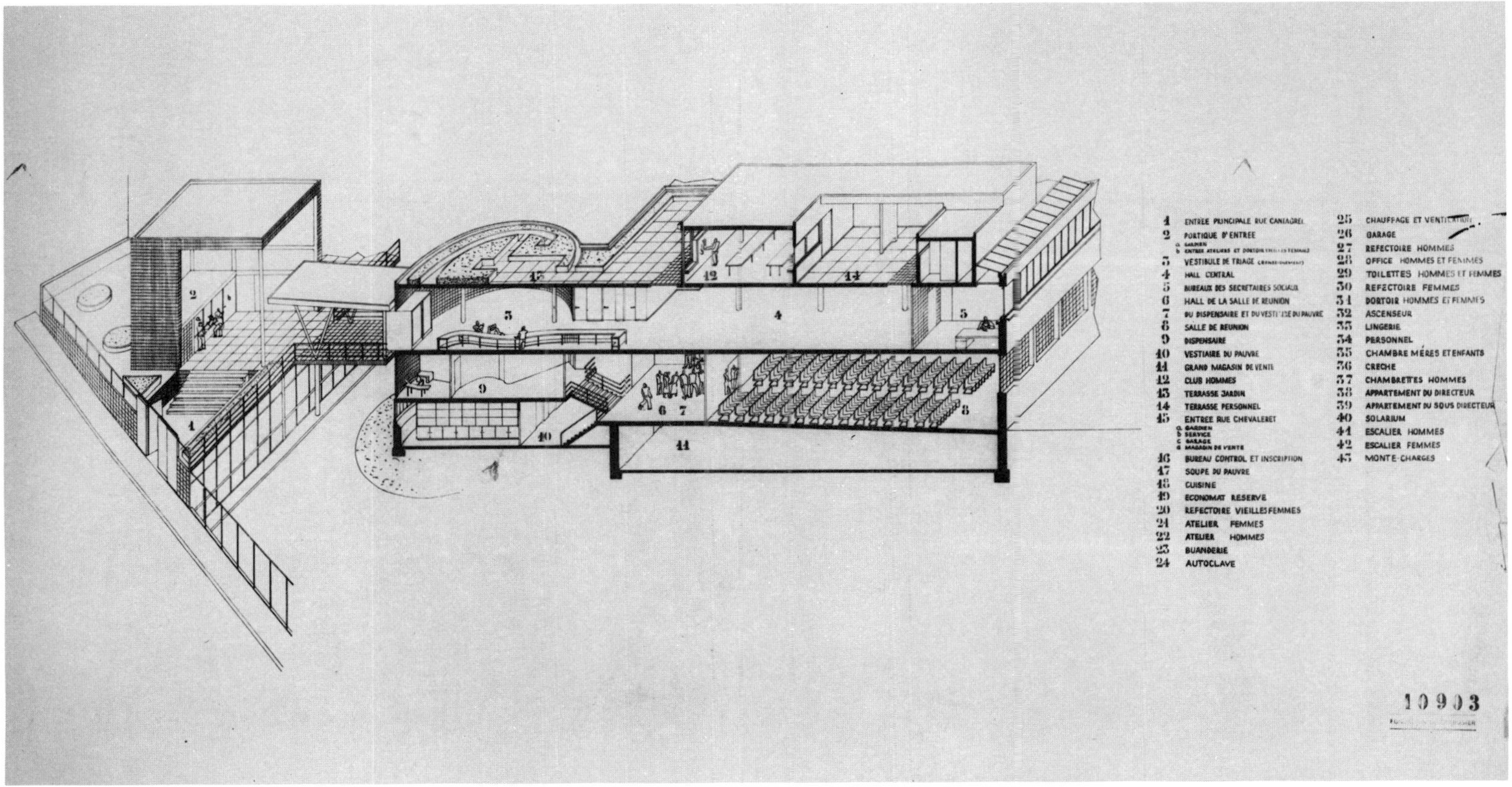

1 ENTREE PRINCIPALE RUE CANTAGREL
2 PORTIQUE D'ENTREE
3 VESTIBULE DE TRIAGE
4 HALL CENTRAL
5 BUREAUX DES SECRETAIRES SOCIAUX
6 HALL DE LA SALLE DE REUNION
7 DU DISPENSAIRE ET DU VESTIAIRE DU PAUVRE
8 SALLE DE REUNION
9 DISPENSAIRE
10 VESTIAIRE DU PAUVRE
11 GRAND MAGASIN DE VENTE
12 CLUB HOMMES
13 TERRASSE JARDIN
14 TERRASSE PERSONNEL
15 ENTREE RUE CHEVALERET
a GARDEN
b SERVICE
c GARAGE
d MAGASIN DE VENTE
16 BUREAU CONTROL ET INSCRIPTION
17 SOUPE DU PAUVRE
18 CUISINE
19 ECONOMAT RESERVE
20 REFECTOIRE VIEILLES FEMMES
21 ATELIER FEMMES
22 ATELIER HOMMES
23 BUANDERIE
24 AUTOCLAVE
25 CHAUFFAGE ET VENTI
26 GARAGE
27 REFECTOIRE HOMMES
28 OFFICE HOMMES ET FEMMES
29 TOILETTES HOMMES ET FEMMES
30 REFECTOIRE FEMMES
31 DORTOIR HOMMES ET FEMMES
32 ASCENSEUR
33 LINGERIE
34 PERSONNEL
35 CHAMBRE MÉRES ET ENFANTS
36 CRECHE
37 CHAMBRETTES HOMMES
38 APPARTEMENT DU DIRECTEUR
39 APPARTEMENT DU SOUS DIRECTEUR
40 SOLARIUM
41 ESCALIER HOMMES
42 ESCALIER FEMMES
43 MONTE-CHARGES
10903

140. Perspective section of the social services building. FLC 10903.

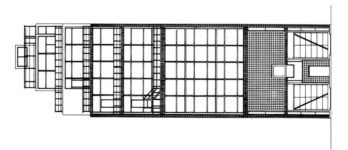

141. Transversal section through the social services building and main building; elevation on the rue du Chevaleret, no. CR 3174.

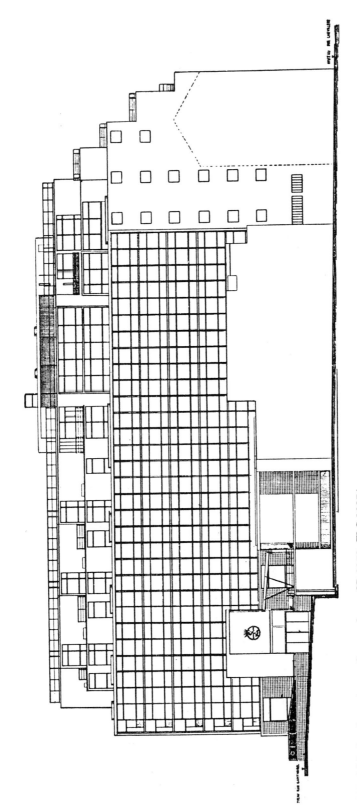

142. Main facade on the rue Cantagrel, no. CR 3173. FLC 10874.

143. Entrance pavilion of the Cité, rue Cantagrel.

144. Entrance pavilion and bridge to the main building.

145. View of the rotunda, the elderly women's dormitory located beneath the entrance portico, and the bridge ("gangway").

146. View of the main facade from the garden terrace of the entrance level.

147. Entrance pavilion and portion of the glass curtain-wall from the roof terrace of the social services.

148. View of the elderly women's dormitory and the entrance pavilion from the lower, pilotis level.

149. View of the vehicle access on the rue du Chevaleret, with the control booth and ramp to the garage. Le Corbusier is seen in the distance.

150. View of the pilotis level and the kitchen facilities.

151. Facade of the Cité de Refuge on the rue du Chevaleret in its original state, with the men's refectory behind the first floor glass brick wall.

52. Rue Cantagrel facade in its original state, showing the "readability" of interior spaces through glass curtain-wall.

153. The Cité just after completion. (From *l'Oeuvre Complete*)

154. Entrance to the rotunda via the bridge or covered "gangway."

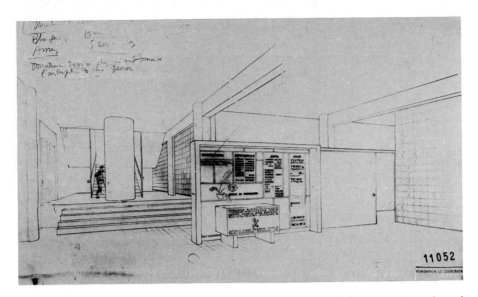

155. Perspective sketch of the main entrance hall with the memorial plaque containing donors' names. FLC 11052.

156. Perspective sketch by Le Corbusier of central hall and stairs.

157. View of the great hall, with the social workers' offices behind the glass bricks, and stairs to the conference hall and the men's lounge.

158. View of the great hall, looking toward the director's office; the rotunda is in the background.

159. View of the orientation and assignment desk at the entry to the rotunda.

160. View of the interior of the rotunda looking toward the great hall.

161. The women's restaurant in its original state.

162. The conference hall with its original decoration.

163. Terrace of the men's lounge and glass curtain-wall of the dormitories. Le Corbusier is in the foreground.

164. A women's dormitory in its original state.

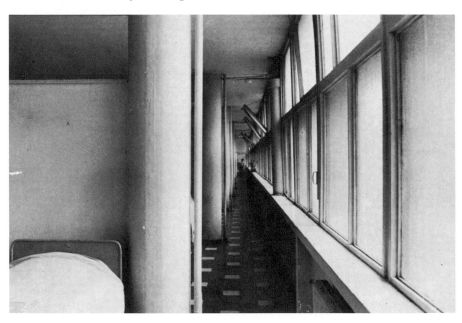

165. A women's dormitory in 1976. (B. Taylor)

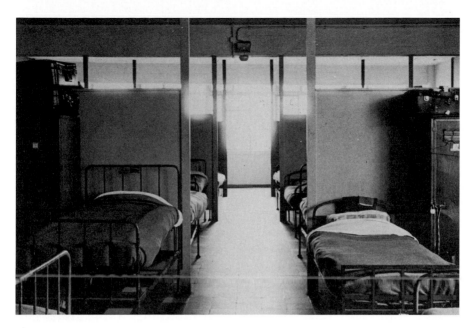

166. View of the interior of men's dormitories in their modified state.

167. View of chambrettes ("boxes") for men in their actual state, 1976.
168. One-half the main stairwell serving the upper levels of the Cité.

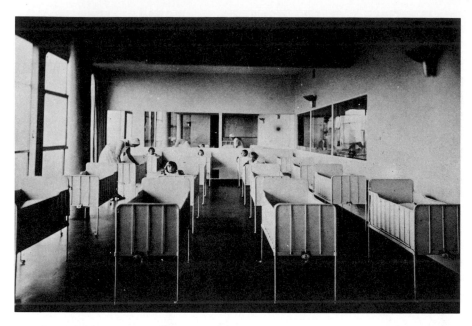

169. The fifth floor crèche in its original state.

170. The playroom in the crèche as it was originally.

171. The room for the Princess de Polignac on the sixth floor.

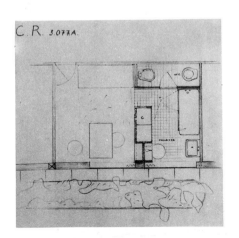

172. Plan no. CR 3077A of the Princess de Polignac's room in the Cité.
173. Perspective sketch of the Princess de Polignac's room.

174. View of the Cité de Refuge in 1986.

175. View of the rooms and terraces on the seventh and eighth floors after restoration.

176. Detail sketch for a portion of the signboard for the Cité. Not executed.

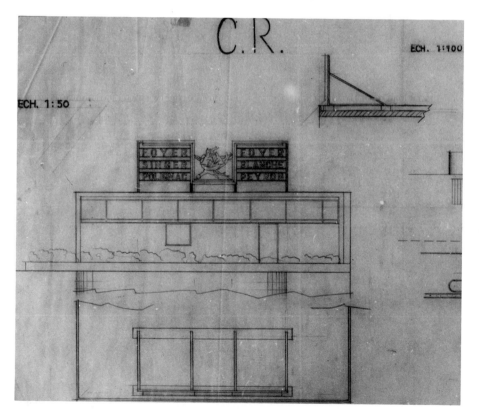

177. Detail of the social services wing and the Salvation Army signboard.

178. Perspective drawing of the entrance from the bridge. CR 2958. FLC 10832.

179. Color study for blue, red, and yellow tiles of entrance portico.

180. Entrance portico as executed in glass mosaic.

181. View of the Cité de Refuge in 1986.

182. View of the Cité de Refuge facade on the rue Chevaleret in 1986.

183. Model (scale 1:100) of Cité de Refuge as it appeared when first built. This was produced in 1987 by Lenon Kaplan and Paul Bonfilio with Norman Baker, Lawrence List, Richard Plowinoki, Robert Platts, Umit Koroglu, Lenon and Sokolowski Studios. Consultant, Brian Brace Taylor. Collection, The Museum of Modern Art, New York. Given in honor of Arthur Drexler by: Lily Auchincloss, Celeste and Armand P. Bartos, Edward and Mary Barnes, Samuel I. Newhouse Foundation, The Joseph H. and Florence A. Roblee Foundation, Skidmore, Owings & Merrill/ New York Partners, Geddes Brecher Qualls Cunningham.

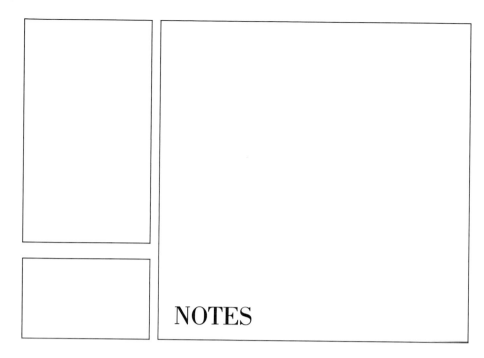

NOTES

■ CHAPTER 1

1. Peter Kropotkin, *Fields, Factories and Workshops* (New York: Harper & Row, 1974; original edition 1899), p. 26.

2. Ebenezer Howard, *Tomorrow, A Peaceful Path to Real Reform* (London, 1898).

3. William Booth, *In Darkest England, and the Way Out* (London: Salvation Army, 1890).

4. George Bernard Shaw, *Major Barbara* (London: Penguin Books, 1973), p. 39.

5. Booth, *In Darkest England*, p. 87.

6. See typescript by Le Corbusier in the CIAM archives, Fondation Le Corbusier (FLC).

7. Le Corbusier, *La Ville Radieuse* (Paris: Editions de l'Architecture d'Aujourd'hui, 1935).

8. Booth, *In Darkest England*, p. 95.

9. Max Weber, *The Protestant Ethic and the Spirit of Capitalism* (London: George Allen and Unwin, 1930).

10. Booth, *In Darkest England*, pp. 140–43.

11. Ibid., p. 152.

12. *En Avant* (Foreword) journal of the Salvation Army in France, Paris, 11 February 1928, p. 2.

13. *En Avant*, 4 August 1928, p. 3.

14. See Roger-H. Guerrand, *Les Origines du Logement Social en France* (Paris: Les Editions Ouvrieres, 1967).

15. *En Avant*, 4 August 1928, p. 3.

16. The present operations of the Cité de Refuge involve a work-aid program, subsidized in part by the city and the state. In 1974 they had 426 men and 46 women

participate in this program; most of them (65 percent) were over forty-five years of age and most (67 percent) stayed for several weeks in the Cité. They included persons recently released from prison (10 percent) or psychiatric hospitals (11 percent) and persons simply classified as vagabonds (79 percent).

17. See Richard F. Kuisel, *Capitalism and the State in Modern France* (Cambridge, 1981).

18. Ibid., p. 101.

19. Ibid., p. 102.

20. Le Corbusier, "La Ville Radieuse," *Plans*, August 1931, p. 12. All translations are the author's, unless otherwise indicated.

■ CHAPTER 2

1. Henry Roberts, *The Dwellings of the Labouring Classes* (London, 1850).

2. Ibid., pp. 26–27, note 2.

3. M. Bouvard, municipal architect, 1890. Archives de la Seine (Asiles).

4. See conclusion.

5. The gradual, rational transformation (renewal) of the surrounding industrial neighborhood was projected by Le Corbusier in mid-1932 when a vast complex of buildings was conceived for adjacent sites to the north and west of the Cité de Refuge, then under construction. A Cité d'Hébergement, or hostel for homeless families, refugees, unemployed, etc., was proposed by the Salvation Army for joint financing with the municipal Services d'Hygiène, Travail et Prévoyance. Numerous preliminary study sketches attest to the importance Le Corbusier attributed to this opportunity for designing collective housing facilities and for introducing a coherent structure into the chaotic surrounding area: rectilinear arrangements of buildings, open green spaces, through-block passageways, etc.

6. Letter, Le Corbusier to Albin Peyron, 3 May 1929. See also the copy of a report by a Salvation Army emissary to Cayenne which was passed on to Le Corbusier. The proposal was to create a hostel, the Maison du Libéré, comprising a commons room, dormitories, restaurant, small workshops, and a placement office to help exconvicts to obtain work. Archives FLC.

7. Unsigned article, with quotations from the inaugural address by Albin Peyron, *Les Temps*, 8 December 1933. See also *Une Cité où Le Pauvre Retrouvera son Chemin*, brochure, 16 pages, published by the Salvation Army in France, no date; text and illustrations by André Labarthe. Contains a list of members of the Army's Comité d'Honneur.

8. Hedwige De Polignac, *Les Polignac* (Fasquelle, 1960), p. 252. We know from drawings that exist at the Fondation Le Corbusier that Le Corbusier designed plans for a villa for the Princess de Polignac in Paris in the mid-1920s, about the same time he received the commission for the annex to the Palais du Peuple, rue des Cordelières.

9. Letter, Albin Peyron to Le Corbusier, 1 August 1929. Archives FLC.

10. See N. A. Miliutin, *Sotzgorod*, ed. G. C. Collins (M.I.T. Press, 1974), for notes concerning the relations between Ginsburg, Miliutin, Gournyi, and Le Corbusier. Also, S. O. Chan-Magomedev, *Moisji Ginsbourg* (Milan: Franco Angeli, 1975). The Narkomfin building was published with plans and photographs in *L'Architecture d'Aujourd'hui* 5 (April–May 1931): 23–27.

11. References to the similarity between the aesthetics of the Cité de Refuge and naval architecture appear in *Les Temps* (see note 7, above).

12. Letter, Le Corbusier to Albin Peyron, 11 October 1930. Archives FLC, box 11/3, items 314–15.

13. Article 2 of the decree dated 13 August 1902, concerning the code on heights of buildings in the city of Paris reads as follows:

For streets less than 12 meters in width, the height may be increased by, but not exceed, 6 meters above the stated official width of the street.

For streets 12 meters in width and wider, the height may only exceed 18 meters by one quarter of the sum by which the street's width exceeds 12 meters; but in no case whatsoever may the height exceed 20 meters above the level of the street.

Archives FLC. For the best explanation of how the heights of buildings in Paris were calculated and the history of the procedure, see "L'évolution des formes urbaines à travers des règlements traditionnels," *Paris-Projet*, revue préparée par l'APUR, nos. 13–14, 1976, p. 24.

14. Handwritten note by Pierre Jeanneret, Archives FLC, item 154.

15. See "A propos du Palais de la Société des Nations," *L'Architecture d'Aujourd'hui* 8 (November 1931): 83–95.

16. Copy of the minutes of the Conseil Général des Bâtiments Civils, meeting of 8 January 1931. Archives FLC, items 206–7.

■ CHAPTER 3

1. Max Weber, *The Protestant Ethic and the Spirit of Capitalism* (London: George Allen and Unwin, 1930).

2. Jules Henrivaux and L. Appert, *La Verrerie depuis vingt ans*, (Paris: E. Bernard, 1894), p. 53.

3. Ibid. Gauthier is a little-known architect who drew up a set of composite plans for the above-mentioned article, in order to illustrate the various applications of glass bricks in a hypothetical glass house.

4. See the excellent article on this dwelling by Kenneth Frampton, "Maison de Verre," *Perspecta 12* (New Haven, 1969), p. 77.

5. "Les Briques Nevada," *Glaces et Verres* 14 (February, 1930).

6. See chapter 4.

7. See, for example, L. C. Boileau's review in *L'Architecture*, 8 August 1903.

8. A. Ducret, "La Cité de Refuge de l'Armée du Salut à Paris," *L'Entreprise française* (25 January 1932): 27.

9. Archives FLC, box 18, items 22–24.

10. The system of calculating the approximate cost of a projected building in cubic meters, rather than square meters, was employed by architects usually at an early phase of a project development when there were great differences in the heights of spaces. It produced a very rough estimate of the cost for a given volume before detailed estimates were made by a professional *métreur* (quantity surveyor).

11. Copy of typewritten contract on letterhead of the Etablissement Quillery, 23 September 1930. Archives FLC, items 357–59.

12. Ibid., p. 3.

13. See Frederick Winslow Taylor, *L'Organisation scientifique du Travail* (Paris: Dunod et Pinet, 1911).

14. This rationalization of the construction process was the logical antecedent to the eventual use of cranes moving along an orthogonal path on rails on the site. The replacement of men by machines in this way was considered an enormous innovation in the post—World War II reconstruction, particularly in the construction of prefabricated mass housing. The influence that cranes of this sort had upon the aesthetic quality of the housing was disastrous.

15. "L'Usine du bien: La Cité de Refuge à Paris," *Le Bâtiment Illustré* (January 1934): 42.

16. Handwritten memorandum by Pierre Jeanneret, Archives FLC, box 7/3, item 127.

17. *Devis descriptif et cahier des charges*, Menuiserie Métallique Moderne of Reims, 3 November 1931, p. 1. Archives FLC box 2/3, items 87—89.

18. See "La Climatisation des Salles de Spectacles, Procédé Tunzini," *L'Architecture d'Aujourd'hui* 8 (1933): 84.

19. Archives FLC, box 1/3.

20. Letter, Dr. Pierre Winter to Le Corbusier, 18 May 1931, Archives FLC.

21. When the architect of the Cité came under attack from the director of the child-care center after the facility had been functioning for several months, he immediately sought expert medical advice concerning child health standards, the ventilation and heating of such facilities, etc. It was undoubtedly at this time that a small book by Dr. Jules Renault, *Un Service moderne de Médecine infantile*, was acquired by Le Corbusier, who then asked its author to visit the Cité de Refuge and give his opinion on the installations.

22. Correspondence between the architect and his client leads one to believe that this was the case for the enterprise Castiaux, responsible for all plumbing and sanitary equipment in the Cité de Refuge.

23. Unsigned article, *Les Temps*, 8 December 1933.

24. Letter, Le Corbusier to the Princess de Polignac, 4 December 1934, Archives FLC.

25. Letter, Le Corbusier to Albin Peyron, 29 January 1935, Archives FLC.

26. Today clients such as the *nouveau rich* princes of Arabia require architects to deposit money in a bank as insurance that the budget and time schedules will be met. Such bonds are one way of discouraging architects from indulging in experiments not provided for in their contract.

27. Most of Le Corbusier's draftsmen worked without pay in the office at the time. (The author's conversations with such former associates as Jean Bossu, Louis Miquel, and others.) It is also interesting to note, the direct influence which the projects in Le Corbusier's office had upon the ideas of his associates. One example of this architectural dissemination is evident in a model for an apartment building with glass facade exhibited by Jean Bossu at the 1931 Salon d'Automne in Paris. See *L'Architecture d'Aujourd'hui* 9 (December 1931): 9.

■ CHAPTER 4

1. Letter, Le Corbusier to the Salvation Army (Colonel Isley), 9 November 1934, Archives FLC, Box 73, item 160.

2. The principal function of presidents of France during this period of history—and particularly President Lebrun—was humorously described as that of officiating at "inaugurations of chrysanthemums" because of their essentially symbolic powers; they spent much of their time at dedication ceremonies while the real power remained in the hands of the president of the *Conseil d'Etat.*

3. Unsigned article appearing in *Les Temps*, 8 December 1933.

4. Letter, Le Corbusier to the Princess de Polignac, 4 December 1934, Archives FLC.

5. Note concerning the visit of Le Corbusier to the Services d'Hygiène des Garnis (to Mr. Ragonet, *rédacteur à la Préfecture de Police*), 16 April 1935. Archives FLC.

6. Letter, Salvation Army to Le Corbusier, 27 December 1933. Archives FLC, box 17, item 118.

7. Note (handwritten) by Pierre Jeanneret on the contacts with the architectural services of the city concerning the mechanical ventilation system. Archives FLC, item 127. No date.

The first authorization to build was given on 24 December 1930. It concerned the first three stories only. The plans submitted to the city included indications for window frames that opened. Mechanical ventilation created a situation that went beyond the scope of the codes which the city architect could not resolve alone. We had to follow the normal channels to obtain a building permit and then defend the mechanical system for ventilation ourselves if the Department of Hygiene raised the issue. The permit for the whole building was given to us on 30 September 1931. . . .

See also letter from the Director of the Plan de Paris, Préfecture de la Seine, to the Salvation Army, 11 May 1935. Box 7/3, item 170.

8. Letter, Director of the Plan de Paris, Préfecture de la Seine, Bureau d'Alignements, to Mr. Huismans, Director General of the Beaux-Arts at the Ministry of National Education, 11 July 1935. Archives FLC, item 91. The latter, an admirer of Le Corbusier, had written to the authorities in Le Corbusier's favor asking that they consider the case of the Cité de Refuge with a benevolent eye.

9. Letter, Salvation Army (Colonel Isely) to Le Corbusier, 12 January 1935. Archives FLC.

10. Copy of a letter from the Director of the Plan de Paris, Préfecture de la Seine, to the Salvation Army, 11 May 1935. Archives FLC, box 7/3, item 170.

11. Letter, Le Corbusier to Gustave Lyon, Acoustical and Ventilating Engineer, 20 September 1934. Archives FLC, item 97.

Dear Friend, . . . I don't know whether you have had the opportunity to see this building (Cité de Refuge) which has gotten a lot of publicity and is visited by people from all over. Here is the reason why I am writing: we have fifty-one rooms for mothers with babies; each room has one glass wall, and the ventilation is by means of forced air. Because the old ladies who are inside can't stick their nose out of the window (i.e., open the window) they pretend they are suffocating. We are nonetheless pumping in thirty-five cubic meters of fresh air an hour in the winter and eighty cubic meters of fresh air in summer into each room. These figures seem high to me, and they ought to insure a perfectly hygienic situation. In spite of this, these ladies raise hell. As a result, the Salvation Army wanted to play a dirty trick on me and put in some fifty windows on my facade, opening onto the outside. . . .

12. Letter from Le Corbusier to Colonel Isely, 9 November 1934. See note 1 above.

13. Letter, Salvation Army to Le Corbusier, 4 May 1935. Archives FLC.

14. The case of the fifty dwellings built at Pessac which remained unoccupied for many months because of a conflict between the municipality and the developer and his architect (Le Corbusier) is one such example. Le Corbusier intervened through his personal acquaintances, Anatole De Monzie and Louis Loucheur, ministers in the government.

15. Letter, Le Corbusier to Senator Justin Godart (former minister), 20 May 1935. Archives FLC, box 7/3, item 82.

16. Letter, J. S. Lavergne, Civil Engineer, to Le Corbusier, 17 May 1935. Archives FLC, box 7/3, items 201–2.

17. Letter, Salvation Army to Le Corbusier, 22 June 1937. Archives FLC.

18. Letter, Bureau Securitas to Le Corbusier, 7 July 1937. Archives FLC, items 28–29.

19. Ibid.

20. See the article by Robert Fishman, "From the Radiant City to Vichy: Le Corbusier's Plans and Politics, 1928–1942," in *The Open Hand*, R. Walden, ed., (Cambridge, Mass.: M.I.T. Press, 1977), pp. 272–79 concerning Le Corbusier's attempts to put his programs into practice with the backing of Pétain's government.

21. These problems had been observed as early as July 1936, when the Salvation Army first wrote to the architects in this regard, and their severity increased with time.

22. Copy of a report from Mr. C. Pean of the Salvation Army to his superior, the Territorial Director, concerning repair of the southern facade, April 1948. Archives FLC.

23. Letter, Le Corbusier to the Commissioner of the Salvation Army, 26 March 1948. Archives FLC.

24. Letter, Pierre Jeanneret to Le Corbusier, 30 April 1948. Archives FLC.

25. See note 22 above.

26. Handwritten memorandum by Le Corbusier concerning the two buildings and the possible development of a standardized sunscreen (*brise soleil*).

27. Letter, Le Corbusier to Wycliffe Booth, head of the Salvation Army in France, 16 October 1951. Archives FLC, items 62–63.

28. Nearly every one of Le Corbusier's clients complained, either orally or in writing, at some time or another of the architect's lack of attention to their own specific problems, manifested—among other ways—by his lecture tours abroad. Henry Fruges, Carlos de Beistigui, and Mr. Plainex are just a few who protested in the late 1920s that it was impossible to see anything fully resolved with their architect. Albin Peyron himself also complained at the time of the Cité de Refuge's conception and execution. Moscow, Rio, Prague, and Algiers were temptations too great to be passed up lightly.

29. Letter, Irène Peyron, Territorial Commissioner of the Salvation Army, to Le Corbusier, 12 August 1952. Archives FLC.

30. In 1975 portions of the Cité de Refuge were classified by the French Ministry of Cultural Affairs as belonging to the national architectural patrimony. This means that they cannot be altered in any way without the approval of the appropriate governmental body; however, it also means that the owners are eligible for (minor) financial aid in restoring these portions.

31. The Salvation Army has consturcted a second center, the Cité de l'Espoir, abutting the Cité de Refuge on the north and facing the rue Chevaleret. The architects were Mr. Verry, architect to the Salvation Army, in association with Mr. Georges Candilis, former assistant to Le Corbusier during the construction of the Unité d'Habitation in Marseille. Architecturally uninspired and devoid of any structural or spatial innovation, the Cité de l'Espoir nevertheless contains single rooms for residents rather than dormitories.

32. However, at least one of his clients, Carlos de Beistigui, whose apartment on the Avenue des Champs-Elysées was renovated by Le Corbusier precisely at the moment the Cité de Refuge was being conceived, encouraged the architect to consider such fields of research. He specifically asked Le Corbusier about a type of glass which permitted the penetration of a maximum amount of heat calories, thereby producing savings in central heating costs.

33. Letter, Le Corbusier to Gustave Lyon, 20 September 1934. See note 11 above.

34. Letter, Mr. Vanderkam of the Salvation Army to Le Corbusier, 4 February 1935. Archives FLC, box 17, item 187. "Some drunkards fighting in the street fell into our glass doors and broke the glass. Would you please look into the matter of replacing the glass once and for all with sheet metal?"

■ CHAPTER 5

1. Michel Foucault, *Surveiller et Punir, Naissance de la prison* (Paris: Gallimard, 1975), pp. 304–5.

2. Ibid., p. 251.

3. Letter, Le Corbusier to Albin Peyron, Archives FLC. Le Corbusier received a typed duplicate of a long report by a Salvation Army representative concerning the situation and needs of exconvicts in the colony. However, no drawings have been found to indicate that Le Corbusier actually made any concrete proposals.

4. Max Weber, *The Protestant Ethic and the Spirit of Capitalism* (London: George Allen and Unwin, 1930), pp. 80, 179–81.

5. Foucault, *Surveiller et Punir*, pp. 245–46.

6. It is interesting and evocative to compare Foucault's discussion of Jeremy Bentham and the importance of *visibility* (of seeing and being seen) in late nineteenth-century doctrines of moral reform, with Le Corbusier's design of an immense, transparent curtain-wall for the Cité, behind which one might perceive, night and day, the movement of persons in their tiny cubicles or in the dormitories. See M. Foucault, "L'oeil du pouvoir" (*entretien*) in *Le Panoptique* (Paris, 1977), p. 18.

7. Alvar Aalto's collaboration, beginning in the early 1930s, with the wood industry in Finland afforded him opportunities to study the potential for prefabrication of building elements in relation to traditional methods of woodworking. With an associate, Mr. H. Bernoulli, he produced extremely detailed studies for joinery in the Villa Mairea for the Gullichsen family, while also working on the factory buildings for the Ahlstrom paper company.

8. See note 17, chapter 1.

9. Manuscript entitled: "The views of Le Corbusier on the Reconstruction of Moscow," 25 October 1930, by S. Gournyi (in French). Archives FLC.